VOLUNTARY ENVIRONMENTAL MANAGEMENT

The Inevitable Future

JOHN MORELLI, PE, Ph.D.

LEWIS PUBLISHERS

Boca Raton London New York Washington, D.C.

Project Editor: Sara Rose Seltzer
Marketing Manager: Barbara Glunn, Jane Lewis, Arline Massey, Jane Stark
Cover design: Dawn Boyd

Library of Congress Cataloging-in-Publication Data

Morelli, John.
Voluntary environmental management : the inevitable future / John Morelli.
p. cm.
Includes bibliographical references and index.
ISBN 1-56670-344-1 (alk. paper)
1. Environmental management. I. Title.
GE300.M67 1999
363.7'05--dc21 98-47480
CIP

Direct all inquiries to CRC Press LLC, 2000 Corporate Blvd., N.W., Boca Raton, Florida 33431.

Lewis Publishers is an imprint of CRC Press LLC

International Standard Book Number 1-56670-344-1
Library of Congress Card Number 98-47480
Printed in the United States of America 1 2 3 4 5 6 7 8 9 0
Printed on acid-free paper

In memory of my father,

John N. Morelli,

June 10, 1907–September 24, 1998

Author

John Morelli is an Associate Professor and has served as Chair of the Department of Environmental Management & Technology at Rochester Institute of Technology (RIT) in Rochester, NY, since 1991. He received a Ph.D. in Environmental Science and an M.S. degree in Environmental Resource Engineering from the State University of New York College of Environmental Science and Forestry, a B.S. in Engineering (Environmental) and Public Affairs from Syracuse University, and has been a Professional Engineer, registered in New York State, since 1984. Prior to his appointment at RIT, he served as Senior Project Manager in the NYS Energy Research and Development Authority (1986 to 1991) and was involved in developing innovative treatment technologies for landfill leachate and contaminated soils at industrial sites. He also did pioneering work in reclaiming landfills. From 1983 through 1986 he was employed by the NYS Department of Environmental Conservation and as a Senior Engineer held responsibility for remedial investigations and corrective actions at state and federal "superfund" sites. Dr. Morelli's current professional interests center around the inevitable need for increased individual responsibility for protection of our environmental, material, and energy resources. He views the recommendations made in this book as a necessary step in that direction.

Contents

Section II A Case for Voluntary Environmental Management

1

Introduction

This book presents a case for the inevitability that environmental management responsibility will shift from the government to the private-sector. In addition, it is a wake-up call to domestic U.S. industries that do not consider themselves part of the international business food chain.

Organization

Section I presents the history of private-sector environmental management over the last quarter century, and reveals how the success of our past strategies for protecting the environment has led to problems for the near- and long-term future. Moreover, environmental management is defined in this section.

Section II draws upon reliable and verifiable information sources from industry, government, and non-governmental environmental organizations in the U.S. to comprehensively identify and describe the deficiencies in the nation's current strategy for protecting the environment through the regulation of industry. It also reveals that in spite of their differences, considerable agreement exists among environmental professionals from these three sectors regarding problems with the current system, the need for more responsibility at the level of the individual, and the desirability of the private-sector taking on more responsibility for protecting the environment. Problems and needs are correlated to the promises and potentials of voluntary environmental performance, which is posited as an alternate and appropriate strategy for entering the 21st century.

Section III explores the process of change in a complex, competitive, and heavily regulated sector of society and will serve as a valuable guide to environmental stakeholders who need to, or wish to, collaborate across sector lines for enhanced and more efficient environmental performance. It constructs an interpretative model that will help readers understand how voluntary environmental actions taken by individuals and individual organizations are influenced by the prevailing social reality and how that reality is in turn effected by individual actions taken.

The Point of Balance

Environmental management activities are derived responses to concerns and requirements existing among the three intersecting spheres of government, the private-sector, and the public. This book is intended as a tool to help environmental stakeholders from all three spheres understand each other and collaborate to develop more efficient and effective programs to protect the environment and sustain the economy. However, while the influences of all three spheres are integrated in this analysis, the center of gravity for most of this work resides in the private-sector.

Overview

Since it first took office, the Clinton Administration has proposed reinventing the U.S. Environmental Protection Agency (EPA) and environmental management in the U.S.[1] Central to the concept of *reinvention* is the recognition that the government has become onerous and inflexible, and that flexibility, good stewardship, and strong partnerships would result in improved environmental performance. Many new voluntary initiatives were launched under this effort.[2] However, an unrelated and unsuccessful attempt by the 104th Congress to dramatically cut back the nation's environmental protection program resulted in a backlash that also had the unfortunate repercussion of temporarily derailing the reinvention initiative.[3] It put *reinvention* of environmental programs on hold while environmentalists rallied to support the environmental protection status quo in this country and to rout the Republican offensive. This sequence of events has obscured the progress of some fairly recent initiatives of industry and states toward the next step in environmental performance, i.e., to get significantly beyond regulatory compliance by marshaling market forces in order to increase pollution control efficiency by integrating it into process design, and to increase overall environmental responsibility of the generators of pollution by integrating environmental management into business management strategies.

EPA now finds itself in an untenable position. On one side, it must contend with the White House, the international business community (including all the large U.S. companies), and a large number of the states insisting upon reform and in fact moving forward with reform, which in some cases is way ahead of EPA's schedule. On the other side, non-governmental environmental organizations (NGOs) are pressuring EPA to withdraw authorization and funding from some very progressive states that have moved in this direction. In order to dispel the charge that EPA's efforts to reform environmental regulations and programs are nothing more than an attempt to rollback 25 years of progress, Administrator Carol Browner has threatened these progressive states with loss of authorization and funding,[4-5] all the while clearly admitting that environmental policy in general, and EPA activities in particular, need to evolve to meet the emerging needs of the 21st century.[6]

EPA is pressured by the administration, states, business, global environmental, and economic movements. Clearly, this is evident in the developed countries, where a more collaborative, efficient, and less costly method of environmental protection holds promise for increased levels of environmental performance. However, EPA is also concerned about maintaining the integrity of its programs during any transition that may take place.

Moving from a command-and-control, enforcement-based, regulatory structure to one that encompasses collaboration among traditional adversaries, requires trust and flexibility as part of a stated policy rather than as something to be used at the discretion of the regulator. Transferring responsibility from government to industry for routine regulatory compliance assurance is not a simple or trivial organizational shift. At one end of the spectrum the path is fairly straightforward: EPA specifies what has to be done and how. At the other end it is more complicated, involving varied and negotiated stakeholder relationships and responsibilities.

EPA *has* recognized the trend towards and acknowledged the benefit of voluntary private-sector environmental performance, and *has* initiated "flexible" programs to accommodate and encourage it.[7] Project XL is the flagship of an armada of EPA's new voluntary programs. However, EPA's interpretation of flexibility is not the same as industry's. For example, Project XL has had difficulties in its implementation phase because regulators are charged with being incapable of letting go of their control of the industry's production process and restricting their concerns to its discharges.[8-13] To circumvent this roadblock, EPA will allow a company to state in its Project XL application a range of alternative actions that a company might choose to take, rather than only the action that it intends to take at that time.[14] In other words, it will allow a company to state that it may use process A under certain circumstances, or process B under other circumstances, and so forth.

EPA sees this as providing the flexibility that companies need in order to be competitive; but this simply is not the case. A company may not know what alternative processes it intends to try, it may be unwilling to make information about those processes public, or it may not be in a position to anticipate the next market demand in its area of endeavor; therefore, this type of flexibility is inadequate. EPA favors the strategy because it fits within its existing command-and-control, enforcement-driven regulatory structure. In reality, it is nothing more than issuing five permits instead of one. For each alternative, companies are required to specify in advance under what conditions they would go from one process to another. As might be expected, this presents a problem. This is where the existing rigid structure and the proposed plan to be flexible do not coincide; it is where the 21st century vision rams squarely into the mid-twentieth century wall.

Voluntary Environmental Management and the ISO 14000

At the conclusion of the Earth Summit held in Rio de Janeiro in 1992, the conference committee asked the International Organization for Standardization, located in Geneva, Switzerland, to consider the need for voluntary international environmental management standards. It did, and in September 1996, ISO 14001, the first of a series of ISO 14000 International Environmental Management Standards was approved.

What does the ISO 14000 bring to the situation described in the preceding section? It brings a system of environmental responsibility, management and compliance that will exist outside of EPA's regulatory structure. Compliance with environmental law and regulation are component parts of the ISO 14000 design criteria for an environmental management system. This is specified under ISO 14001, the ISO standard that sets forth the criteria for establishing an appropriate environmental management system (EMS), and under which an organization's EMS will be evaluated and certified. Compliance with all applicable environmental regulatory requirements is a stated goal of the ISO 14001 EMS standard, but the ISO 14001 EMS is not a performance standard. It does not ask the question: "Is the environmental regulation requirement being met?" Rather, it asks: "Does the organization have a system in place capable of meeting the requirement?"; "Does it have a system in place that appropriately measures progress toward meeting that requirement?"; "Do the results of that measurement indicate that significant progress toward meeting that requirement is being made?"; "Are there sufficient, adequate, and timely means for correcting situations or events that violate environmental law or regulation; and, "Is there a process in place to review the EMS in view of its success in achieving its goals and revise it accordingly if it is not?"

Industry designed the ISO 14001; EMS has ownership of it and is encouraging its implementation around the world. In Europe, within a month of final approval of the EMS standard, the 15 state members of the European Union voted unanimously to adopt it as the European standard.[15] Individual national standards like the BS 7750 will be phased out and replaced with ISO 14001. In Japan, the Ministry of International Trade and Industry has directed, or strongly recommended, that its companies become ISO 14001 certified in order to remain competitive and increase market share.[16] In the U.S., Lucent Technology has worked with EPA to develop a pilot project under Project XL to test the ISO 14001 system as an alternative to the current government-initiated, command-and-control system.[17] In addition, a number of states have formed a task force to collaboratively conduct and evaluate pilot programs to assess how ISO 14001 can be incorporated into existing state programs.[18] EPA's Office of Enforcement and Compliance Assurance

(OECA) in Washington, D.C. has formed a task force of 31 members, with 15 to 17 state departments of environmental protection represented, to evaluate ISO 14000 and determine how it might fit into EPA's program.[19]

This research asserts that the ISO 14001 environmental management system standard and its complementary ISO 14000 series components will form an alternative structure for ensuring environmental compliance and responsibility. It also maintains that demonstration of increased environmental performance and widespread adoption of this standard by industry will draw to it a significant portion of what EPA now sees as its exclusive domain of responsibility. This proposition is consistent with some obvious projections for the future. For example, it is reasonable to project that we will move away from solutions that focus on treating waste rather than preventing its generation because this approach is inefficient. The inefficiency is inherent in the design of such end-of-the pipe solutions. End-of-pipe technologies are not part of the original integrated production process design. Such pollution control technology was adapted afterwards; thus, while it may be adequate for removing gross pollution, it becomes dramatically inefficient at removing more subtle levels of pollution. In order to move to the next phase of environmental protection, the production process must be reinvented. This involves new considerations in means of production, selecting materials, designing products, and designing processes that use materials. These all are components of the next generation of environmental enhancement. Moving upstream in the production process moves away from areas of government expertise and into industry's intellectual and experiential realm.

The significant point is that government cannot provide all the answers, for it does not have all the information. Therefore, it cannot walk into every industry and tell them how to modify their production processes to effectively minimize pollution, at least not in ways that will keep the U.S. means of production sharply competitive. In a world where the U.S. has become a player rather than the master of ceremonies this is a critical consideration. In order to be more competitive in the global market, U.S. industries need to be able to respond quickly to marketplace demands. In order for the government to provide industry with such freedom, industry needs to embrace environmental responsibility as its own and demonstrate that it is capable of handling it. ISO 14000 is a tool used by industry both to drive and to demonstrate its environmental performance. EPA would be well advised to take advantage of the enormous resource being voluntarily pledged.

Additionally, as a member of the World Trade Organization and in accordance with Section 12 of the National Technology Transfer Act, the U.S. government is obligated to give preferential consideration to the use of international voluntary standards as a primary step in developing regulation. Under OMB Circular A-119, all U.S. federal agencies have been required since 1979 to have a voluntary standards executive. In 1990, EPA was the only major agency that did not have one and that did not belong to the American National Standards Institute, principally because it did not recognize the term "voluntary" as having any relevance to its function.[20] While EPA now is represented, and while many within the Agency do recognize the need for and benefit of voluntary environmental performance, there remains a very formidable cultural inertia in an organization that traditionally has none.

ISO 14000 has the potential to provide environmental management functions that parallel portions of EPA's existing regulatory activities in areas where the Agency has been criticized for being ineffective or inefficient. This development can provide EPA with a perhaps otherwise unattainable opportunity for a smooth transition away from its outdated strategies. The Agency needs to support the ISO 14000 development without adding onerous burdens by trying to fit any or all of it into existing regulatory programs. If EPA chooses to resist, the adoption of ISO 14000 in this country might be diminished, resulting in adverse economic impacts, both for our transnational corporations and our domestic companies who are not paying a lot of attention to this development because they do not see themselves as part of the *international food chain.*

It must be recognized that much of the strategy behind EPA's varied efforts to reinvent itself is based on the notion of shared and expanded responsibility. A question that needs to be asked is: "Can EPA promote expanded private-sector responsibility without providing true empowerment?" EPA has proposed to meet with the Environmental Council of States to discuss enhancements to its partnership programs.[21] Yet, the states are wary that these will not be partnerships at all but rather an opportunity for EPA to get them all in a room at the same time to tell them the way its going to be. It is the premise of this work that EPA has to let go of some of its control or this vision cannot work.

Finally, if EPA either through its action or lack of action impedes voluntary private-sector efforts, or is perceived by the public to be obstructing implementation of voluntary programs and actions that will enhance environmental quality, it will find itself increasingly needing to defend this questionable position while industry enjoys the distinction of holding the high moral ground. This work asserts also that this would be an untenable position for an agency charged with protecting the environment and suggests that ISO 14000 can advance EPA's "reinvention" efforts by providing a crucial and requisite voluntary environmental management component to society's overall "system" for protecting the environment.

Section I

The History and Definition of Environmental Management

2

The History and Evolution of Environmental Management in the U.S.

Experience, the universal Mother of Sciences.

— *Miguel de Cervantes, 1605*

It can be argued that the history of environmental management in the U.S. spans more than a century. From about 1890 to the middle of the 20th century, environmental management issues focused on the proper use of land resources and the importance of maintaining natural areas. This period of environmental management history may be appropriately dubbed the "Land Preservation Era." Publication of Rachel Carson's book *Silent Spring* in 1962, marked the conception of a second era of environmental management. Carson's exposé of the excessive use of pesticides in the U.S. elevated national awareness and concern and gave rise to the "Pollution Control and Cleanup Era," which can be said was launched ceremoniously on April 22, 1970 – the first Earth Day. The efforts of the two decades that followed produced substantial environmental quality improvements across the U.S. and dramatically expanded the base of knowledge of environmental impacts. Issues of responsibility and accountability were brought to the forefront during this time by a series of environmental calamities, both here and abroad. The ultimate fate of waste materials became firmly established as the responsibility of the generator, and waste-generating organizations came to realize that compliance with current environmental laws might not suffice to protect their assets against related future liabilities. This evolution of knowledge and thought gave rise to the third and current era of environmental management, "The Era of Global Environmental Responsibility."

In this third era, the private-sector acknowledges environmental responsibility as a legitimate part of doing business. Environmental management is elevated from the operational level to include a significant strategic component. Multinational corporations and other organizations with significant international business interests assess their environmental impacts abroad as well as at home.

Environmental Management: Circa 1970

Many of the initiatives taken by industry in the early 1990s toward environmental self-regulation had their roots in the concerns of leaders of industry during the early 1970s. At that time, industry found itself in a difficult position. On the one hand, it could see that a need existed for some control over the increasing levels of pollution, and on the other, it was obligated to remain competitive. A debate revolved around what were appropriate roles for the public, government, and industry regarding environmental protection and the extent to which industry needed to become more socially responsible. Lacking national environmental quality standards, not only was it difficult for industry to set and achieve relevant environmental performance goals and targets, but the cost of doing so put a company intent on improving its environmental performance at a disadvantage with respect to competitors who had no regulatory incentives to do the same. Within industry there was a trend toward establishing environmental control executives, groups, and departments. There was a call for the creation of a new discipline that would provide a bridge between sciences and social concerns.

A Call for National Standards

By 1970, it was obvious that air pollution was impacting a variety of systems and the proposed new Air Quality Act of 1967 was being heralded by regulators as a call to the business community to assume responsibility for its impacts on the nation's atmosphere.[22]

M.A. Wright, President of the U.S. Chamber of Commerce and Chairman of the Board of Humble Oil Refining Company, stated that business could not afford to *not* assume this responsibility voluntarily when the obvious alternative was for Congress to mandate actions likely to be more costly and less efficient than otherwise necessary.[23] He proposed that business take on this charge while it still had the freedom to act. John T. Middleton, Director of the National Center for Air Pollution Control, sympathized with M.A. Wright's concern that business needed to voluntarily implement effective pollution abatement programs but did not agree that industry was free to make a reasoned and resolute response to the problem.[24] Without that freedom he did not think it realistic to expect voluntary implementation of pollution abatement programs. Middleton was concerned about the lack of incentives for the operator to control pollution and said:

> Since under our present laws, a state or city that starts up an effective control program is more often than not asking its industries to take on a competitive disadvantage, the disinclination in industry boardrooms to control pollution is also felt in the chambers of government where there is understandable concern — not only with the air citizens breathe, but also with the source of their employment. If we accept this analysis of the

> conflict, then it's apparent that what emerges is a need for air pollution standards that can be applied universally and equitably. Without such standards, industry is not free to make a reasoned and resolute response to the problem of air pollution but is shackled to the horns of a dilemma. It needs to maintain its place as a responsible segment of society, as Mr. Wright suggests, but it also needs to maintain its competitive position in the marketplace.

Middleton called for industry to support the establishment of minimal national emission standards. At the time, the responsibility for establishing standards was assigned to state and local governments.

Regulators argued that while business was being called upon to act responsibly, it could not be trusted to act with complete freedom because generators of pollution lacked adequate incentives to control it properly. The lack of uniform environmental standards from state to state, or even from city to city, guaranteed that any efforts taken by government or industry to improve the environment would serve to disadvantage the participating businesses by imposing costs not borne by less responsible competitors or competitors living in other jurisdictions. Therefore, from the perspectives both of industry and government, national standards presented the only realistic approach to reducing pollution.

A New Type of Professional

It was becoming apparent that environmental concerns were so numerous and complicated that the existing business management infrastructure could not adequately support the associated needs. In response to this concern, David Sarnof, Chairman of RCA, called for the creation of a new professional: *manager of environmental forces.*[25] He felt that there was a need to unify technology design and application with its impacts on human and natural environments. He envisioned this professional serving as a counselor to government and industrial decision-makers at local, national, and international levels. Management of environmental forces would draw upon a broad range of disciplines, gradually developing its own discipline-specific characteristics and eventually contributing to education by bridging natural sciences, social sciences, and the humanities.

Investment in Pollution Control R&D

The slower than anticipated growth of nuclear power resulted in an accelerated growth in fossil fuel-fired power plants, as well as tremendous increases in sulfur oxide emissions,[26] driving the government to look to industry for help in developing and demonstrating pollution reduction techniques on a large-scale basis. The petroleum and chemical industries rose to the occasion and began to devote resources to research and development efforts to reduce pollution, particularly sulfur oxide pollution.

The Environmental Movement

The repercussions of the Vietnam War were evident in the lack of public trust in government and industry with regard to the environment. The environmental movement was described by Denis Hayes in 1970 as, "... a movement of working men, who are breathing poison every day in the mines and mills, who raise their children downwind of the smoke-belching factories."[27] A strand of the movement professed a distrust of regulatory agencies and politicians and made demands directly to corporations that they begin to consider people's lives and the environment. The movement used stock proxy fights, lawsuits, demonstrations, research, and elections as tactics to force industry to pay more attention to these demands.

Regarding Allocation of Responsibility

Herbert D. Doan, President of Dow Chemical, claimed we need both public and private action to provide solutions to environmental problems, but explained that although these problems could be solved by industry, it was not the responsibility of industry to create policies about appropriate levels of environmental quality.[28] He suggested a clearinghouse to help develop an image of what the nation wanted and what was valued and then to provide opportunities for individual participation. He proposed the following:

> It is the place of concerned people to advocate changes in our value systems and our mores so that we can act on such problems as pollution control. It is the responsibility of the citizens to sort out these problems and ask for solutions to the most pressing. It is the responsibility of the government to respond to these pressures with timely reordering of national priorities — and to establish policy with rules and regulations. It is the responsibility of industry to create products and services within the limits of government policy and public attitudes.

Doan explained also that industry functions on a profit basis and it was incorrect to believe that it would solve any problems without a customer for that solution. He suggested that if a market in environmental control could be defined, then the marketplace would take care of that need automatically.

Edgar B. Speer, President of U.S. Steel, agreed that the profit incentive is the best instrument for accomplishing whatever it is that needs to be accomplished.[29] He called for collaboration between government and industry to develop guidelines as an appropriate alternative to government-directed punitive measures. He charged that the U.S. needed to get away from the notion that environmental progress could be achieved only by diminishing the nation's production, and complained that regulators needed to stop changing regulations and give everyone a reasonable opportunity to comply before further changes were considered. Existing plant equipment conformed to pollution standards when it was installed and constantly changing regulations required large investments of capital and labor resources to comply.

A New Agency

Also in 1970, a new federal agency called the Environmental Protection Agency (EPA) was created that would combine jurisdiction for air, water, and solid waste programs all under one roof.[30] Some in industry looked forward to this consolidation as likely to standardize procedures for managing environmental issues.

Environmental Management: Circa 1980

By 1980, industry was enmeshed in an ever-increasing web of environmental regulation and developing policy. New concepts like *cradle-to-grave* responsibility and *strict, joint and several, and retroactive* liability were adding serious levels of complexity to regulatory compliance efforts. Consumers and investors were sending messages through the marketplace that environmental protection was important to them. Companies were being forced to think about more than just how to meet a specified emission limit. But then for awhile during the early years of the Reagan administration, the message changed. Industry, confused by the disparity between administration policy and environmental regulation, adopted a wait-and-see attitude. By the mid-1980s in the wake of the death of thousands in Bhopal, India as a tragic result of a chemical leak from a Union Carbide Plant, industry resumed its movement toward environmental responsibility with a marked paradigm shift from pollution "control" to pollution "prevention."

Simultaneously, environmental management was developing as an increasingly important and empowered, multi-faceted discipline. Environmental managers functioned at the interfaces among science, technology, economics, law, and ethics. Often viewed within the industry as harbingers of additional costs and restrictions, they sought to create incentives to induce action.

Assuming Responsibility

In response to numerous lawsuits filed against the Allied Chemical Company for damages resulting from its improper and illegal discharge of one of its chemical products, Kepone, into the James River in Virginia, Allied incorporated the concept of *environmental responsibility* into its new incentive-compensation plan and developed and implemented new procedures for monitoring the environmental decision-making of plant personnel.[31] This is particularly interesting because the mismanagement of this suspect carcinogen, Kepone, was the responsibility of Life Science Products, a subcontractor of Allied. It was the first time that a company had been held responsible for the actions of a subcontractor. Allied stopped Kepone production, and industry was alerted that environmental responsibility did not necessarily stop at its fenceline.

Changing Consumer Profiles

Private-sector concern over economic impacts moved beyond regulatory fines and health-related liability, and entered the arena of competition for market share when consumption behavior analyses revealed that environmentally responsible target markets were becoming increasingly significant and warranted development of environment-oriented consumer affairs or marketing programs.[32]

Concerns About Waste Disposal

The cradle-to-grave concept of responsibility established by the Resource Conservation and Recovery Act of 1976 and the strict, joint and several, retroactive liability created under the Comprehensive Environmental Responsibility, Compensation and Liability Act of 1980 (a.k.a. Superfund) contributed to the conclusion by industrial environmental managers that hazardous waste disposal would be their biggest problem in the years to come.[33]

Environmental management strategy received much criticism for being little more than a *shell game*, just moving contaminants around among air, water, and soil media. Costs of compliance were considered to be excessive and inflationary, and industry felt compelled to incinerate wastes as an alternative to landfilling them in order to minimize future liability.

The Dark Ages

In the early 1980s, the Reagan administration attempted to reduce the burden of environmental regulations on industry by backing off from the agency's earlier, more aggressive approach toward enforcement. Reagan acted through his appointed EPA Administrator Ann (Gorsuch) Burford and her subordinate Rita M. Lavelle. The lack of enforcement action caused confusion in the regulated community regarding the best course of action. During these years, industry adopted a wait-and-see attitude with respect to environmental compliance.

A Tragic Reawakening: Bhopal and a Paradigm Shift

The public rejected attempts to weaken EPA, and the subsequent firing of EPA's Rita M. Lavelle and the resignation of EPA Administrator Anne M. Burford sent a clear message to industry that the administration's efforts to weaken environmental requirements were over. But it may have been the Bhopal tragedy that played the pivotal role in restarting the movement toward more responsible environmental management. It was responsible for initiating a shift of emphasis in industry from remedial, technically-based environmental programs to preventive, socially based programs. Industry, particularly the chemical industry, began initiating voluntary programs to prevent such tragedies from occurring in the future.

> *History teaches us that men and nations behave wisely once they have exhausted all other alternatives.*
>
> — *Abba Eban*

Environmental Management: Circa 1990

By 1990, clear evidence emerged that voluntary environmental programs could not only reduce liability, but also produce economic gain. The 3M Corporation's slogan, *Pollution Prevention Pays,* caught the attention of many large private–sector companies. The costs associated with environmental regulatory compliance are now not just an *excessive annoyance* to many companies, but are becoming accepted as normal costs of doing business. The quality standards of ISO 9000 are driving managers to look at environmental costs in the same way they would any other costs. Consequently, leading industries are elevating environmental management from an operational function to a strategic function, and are developing environmental visions, mission statements, and codes of ethics. In order to ensure that they meet these commitments, some companies require their business partners (e.g., suppliers, distributors, etc.) to live up to specified environmental requirements. In many cases, these requirements may be at least as effective at improving private-sector environmental performance as are government regulations.

The national environmental quality standards that industry called for 20 years earlier are in place and well established. Although these standards do not provide an absolutely level playing field for all involved, they provide enough balance and consistency to assure private-sector environmental decision-makers that their treatment by regulatory agencies is not completely arbitrary. With this assurance, industry is better positioned to initiate more self-directed initiatives to protect the environment.

Environmental responsibility is now assigned to the highest administrative levels in all major U.S. corporations. Environmental managers find themselves no longer stationed only at the end-of-the-pipe, but often upstream in the production process. As environmental management becomes more integrated into the business management structure, environmental managers increasingly become part of trans-disciplinary management teams.

Socially Responsible Investing

Justification for the upward mobility of the environmental manager in business is supported by traditional business values. Socially responsible investment has become a means of expressing philosophical preference and protest,[34] and environmental responsibility is included among the major social responsibilities identified by investors. Social responsibility provides a potentially rewarding selection criterion for investors. Surveys show that investments in socially sensitive stocks over the 5 year period from 1984 to 1988, returned 31 percent more than Standard & Poor.[35] Selection criteria for social responsibility include: limited business (less than 4 percent) in weapons, alcohol, tobacco, gambling, and nuclear power, environmental responsibility, compliance with worker safety regulations, and fair treatment of employees. There is a developing trend among investment companies toward more socially responsible funds.

Citizen Suits

Market-based incentives for complying with environmental regulation are not the only public drivers. By bestowing legal standing upon the public, thereby allowing it to sue in order to enforce public environmental enforcement responsibilities, Congress has amplified the potency of legislative provisions that empower courts to order a company to provide financial relief for environmental restoration.

Voluntary and Self-Imposed Environmental Policies

Public power utilities have included environmental responsibility as a building block for, and a requisite part of, the development process for every policy they create.[36] DuPont Canada has developed an environmental policy that establishes its environmental principles and goals[37] to include waste reduction in its manufacturing processes, reuse waste materials from existing operations, and recycle waste plastics and other waste materials. DuPont is investing in research to increase production efficiency and to make products more environmentally benign. Environmental communication strategies are being developed or enhanced in order to help consumers make informed choices and to get the word out about what is being accomplished at DuPont.

The Coalition for Environmentally Responsible Economies (CERES) works to persuade companies to develop responsible corporate environmental policies based upon ten principles symbolically called the *"Valdez Principles."*[38] Industry response has been varied and there has been a considerable amount of resistance to the requirement that participants must develop and make available a comprehensive annual environmental assessment report card.

Environmental Management as a Strategic Management Function in Industry

A study performed by Deloitte & Touche and the Stanford University Graduate School of Business, reveals that American businesses are acknowledging the relationship between their future success in the marketplace and public perception regarding their environmental performance.[39] The study reports that regulatory issues continue to dominate environmental concerns and activities in business. Associated costs have evolved during the period of 1973 to 1990, from an *"excessive annoyance"* to a normal business cost. Seventy-five percent of the companies surveyed had paid penalties for violations of environmental regulations. Average fines were as high as $300,000.

Two-thirds of companies expected more stringent environmental regulations in the future. Well over 90% of the responders held environmental issues as important strategic considerations. The researchers claimed that what the study revealed was that "companies are transitioning [away from regulatory compliance as the principal motivator] to proactive environmental policies." The transition was thought to be in its infancy but being driven quickly into the heart of financial and strategic plans by consumer and regulatory pressures.

Of those responding to the survey:

- ❑ 31% had policies on recycling
- ❑ 26% had policies on energy conservation
- ❑ 25% had policies on environmental image issues
- ❑ 20% were involved in green labeling

Since 1973, environmental expenditures had grown from an "expensive annoyance" to a normal cost of doing business. Regulatory compliance will continue to lead corporate environmental concerns. New and increasingly sophisticated marketing programs are being initiated as environmental strategies evolve. Companies face four critical challenges in the management of their environmental strategy:

- ❑ regulatory compliance
- ❑ environmental risk management
- ❑ marketing response
- ❑ integration of environmental strategies

Therefore, consumer and competitive market forces are moving environmental issues to the heart of American business strategy.

Industrial Environmentalism

A global community concern for the environment is beginning to develop.[40] In industry, this concern is being manifested by developing, publicizing, and adhering to environmental visions, missions, and codes of ethics. An increase in environmental responsibility is predicted as one of the ten essential paradigms of a new way of thinking that will lead us into a prosperous period through the '90s and into the early 21st century.[41] Other related paradigms for the future include: peace as a pragmatic necessity and an altruistic reality, increased international cooperation, and increased democratic free enterprise.

Industry is trying conduct business without damaging the environment in order to restore its credibility with the public.[42] Sensitivity to environmental concerns is increasing, and tolerance for environmental risks is decreasing. Companies are beginning to discover that good environmental performance can yield dividends in avoided costs as well as recognition as environmentally responsible corporate citizens.[43] Manufacturers are increasingly involved in joint recycling ventures, waste minimization, substitution of toxic chemicals, waste treatment, and reduction of the use of chlorofluorocarbons.

Driven by the increasing availability and accessibility to the public of industry-specific environmental information, pressure on industry to become more environmentally responsible is predicted for the next decade.[44] One challenge will be to encourage customers to participate in sharing environmental responsibilities.

3

Defining Management

> *Management is work, and as such it has its own skills, its own tools, its own techniques ... Management is the organ, the life-giving, acting, dynamic organ of the institution ... Without the institution there would be no management. But without management there would also be only a mob instead of an institution.*
>
> *Peter Drucker**

In order to build a comprehensive understanding of the term "voluntary environmental management" it is important to begin with a foundational definition of "management." Most environmental professionals working today have not had formal academic preparation in the concepts and theories of management. Though some have attended management seminars or internal management training, it is most often the case that the topics being presented at such events address the specific *how-to* elements of management, rather than broader issues focusing on what management is, or what it is supposed to be. Additionally, in many cases management training opportunities have been provided only to individuals with supervisory responsibilities. Since traditionally the role of the environmental professional has been to react to specific environmental problems of the various units within an organization rather than to design and manage organization-wide environmental management systems, this lack of preparation has not presented an insurmountable obstacle. In view of the current and continuing demand for increased overall production efficiency and higher quality environmental performance, such systems now are necessary and a deeper understanding of management and management systems is warranted.

There are many interesting works on the topic of management and much of the variation among them deals with the dimensions of management, how various elements of management (e.g., techniques, functions, resources, etc.) are categorized and labeled, philosophies of management, expectations regarding employees and employee performance, and how the organization is viewed. This work does not attempt to argue in support of one variation or another, nor to improve on any, but rather it borrows from and builds upon a few in order to construct a customized definition that will be meaningful for the discussion at hand.

* Drucker, Peter. *Management: Tasks, Responsibilities, Practices.* Harper & Row, New York, 1973.

Dimensions and Elements of Management

The fundamental basis of management theory is founded upon the observation that there are some common managerial elements that are identifiable across a diversity of applications. These elements may be categorized in a variety of ways, including by types of technique applied at the operations level, and by general functions at the organizational level. Some developmental highlights of each of these characterizations are introduced below and briefly discussed in relation to environmental management.

Techniques at the Operations Level: Observe, Measure, and Compare

At the end of World War II, Frederick Taylor originated the Scientific Management school-of-thought.[45] Taylor believed that the application of scientific methods to production management would increase efficiency. He identified observation, measurement, and experimental comparison as the principal scientific methods applicable to management.

Originally, these methods were used by scientific managers to standardize worker tasks, develop production performance standards, and establish related systems of wage incentives. By the 1960s, scientific management methods were broadly applied in business organizations. Today, such methods occupy a significant part of the effective environmental manager's toolbox. Measurement has become of paramount importance, and the now commonly heard adage, "If you can't measure it, you can't control it," is an important element in current environmental management approaches. The assumption is that if you cannot measure *it*, you will not know what *it* is doing and may not even know whether *it* exists. This could lead to disaster for an environmental manager and his or her organization. Observation is also an essential part of today's environmental management strategy. It is how we find out what is there and what needs to be controlled, and therefore measured.

Taylor's practice of comparing one worker's methods to another's in order to find the best way to do a job and develop performance standards for that activity, may have provided the underpinning of cross-organizational benchmarking and identification of best practices in use today. It is important in this sense, to recognize that all production systems use variations of the same unit processes and operations (e.g., cutting, grinding, distilling, drying, filtering, etc.). It follows logically that what works to reduce environmental releases for a specific unit operation in one production system may be applicable to a similar operation in another very different type of system. There is willingness among many organizations to share information regarding their environmental management successes. Effective environmental managers capitalize on this opportunity by establishing and maintaining communications with their counterparts in such organizations.

Functions at the Organization Level

Henry Fayol, a contemporary of Taylor, approached management at the level of the organization.[46] He identified six general activities of organizations, of which management was one, and five management functions including: planning, organizing, directing, controlling, and coordinating. Fayol held that these functions of management were common among all organizations. While different authors have varied in their identification and characterization of management functions, the functional approach has been acknowledged as valid by a large number of authors in the field. The majority have adopted the first four of Fayol's functions, and some have split his *organizing* function into two separate functions, *organizing* and *staffing*. For the purposes of this book, management activities are categorized into five distinct functions including: planning, organizing, staffing, directing, and controlling. The reader should note that the activities associated with each of these functions may overlap or be contained within the others. For example, it may be necessary to organize a planning committee or to plan a reallocation in staffing. However, for the purpose of clarity, it will be helpful to think of these five functions as sequential and discrete phases.

Planning

Planning is the first functional activity in management. Planning establishes goals and thereby delineates the parameters that managers need to identify. These include:

- tasks that need to be performed in order to achieve identified goals
- resources that need to be secured in order to perform specified tasks [There are seven categories of resources that are essential to management. These include: human resources, organizational resources, financial resources, material resources, energy resources, environmental resources, and informational resources. The relative proportion of each may vary from one project to another but all tend to be present in every effort.]
- standards against which performance must be measured in order to determine when goals have been reached

These four activities (i.e., establishing goals, identifying tasks, identifying resource needs, and setting standards of progress) comprise the main body of the planning function. In addition to the specification of goals, tasks, resource needs, and performance standards, planning phase outputs include specifying:

- resources to be used
- locations within the organization at which the plan will be carried out

- ❑ level of authority at which the planned activity will function
- ❑ organizational modifications necessary to implement the plan

Organizing

Organizing involves assembling and allocating the resources that were specified in the planning phase (e.g., this might include funds for salaries, specified leaders, workspaces, etc.). It is the step in which responsibility is assigned and authoritative relationships are established. Acting on direction provided during the planning phase, organizational structures are modified or new organizational structures are created in the organizing phase. Additional organizing phase outputs may include specified skill requirements.

Staffing

The staffing function determines and procures the specific human resources and training needed to provide the organization with the staff and skill sets it needs to implement planned and organized activities successfully. It is concerned with attracting and keeping good people.

Directing

Directing is where the day-to-day management takes place. It involves moving the organization toward its goals and objectives through appropriate elements of leadership including:

- ❑ building a good working climate
- ❑ communicating expectations
- ❑ actively listening to organization members
- ❑ building on individual strengths
- ❑ providing motivation to work toward goals

"Directing" is the dynamic implementation of the plan.

Controlling

Controlling involves the measurement of performance, the comparison of actual performance with established standards, the analysis of discrepancies, and the taking of associated corrective actions. From a quantitative perspective, controlling is concerned with what is getting done, and is linked with the meeting of goals and objectives. Qualitatively, it deals with how things are getting done, and is linked with leadership.

Upwards Influence and Nested Functions

It should be clear that feedback and upward influence exists at each functional level. For example, if measurements conducted as a controlling function activity reveal that discrepancies exist with respect to projected outputs, a response at the directing level may be necessary to remedy the situation. It may be the case, however, that the expectations set forth in the original plan are unrealistic; in such a case, modifications in planning may be called for. Alternatively, it may be determined that staff skills are inadequate and additional training is needed — a staffing function. In the final analysis, effective management is a flexible and integrated multi-phase process that solicits, encourages, and is responsive to multidirectional flows of information.

Also, as mentioned earlier, it is important to recognize that in each management function there exists elements of other management functions. For example, a unit leader who decides to redirect the unit's allocated resources (a unit-level organizing activity) in order to meet a new production deadline, does not make this change without first determining an appropriate course of action (a unit-level planning activity). Yet, at the unit level, this is part of the directing function. It may be useful in making the distinction to think of these functions as beginning with upper- or lower-case letters.

*P*lanning, *O*rganizing, and *S*taffing are those formal activities associated with significant modifications or new commitments. At the corporate or division levels, they may include activities like 5 year planning, organizational restructuring, downsizing, or expanding the workforce. At the business unit or production line level, they may include implementation of new processes, unit organization restructuring, choosing to replace a retiring worker with an individual with a different set of skills, or setting production and safety goals beyond those established by the parent organization. *D*irecting, with a big "D," may involve establishing corporate policies on rewarding individual innovation, or at the unit level, staff reassignments within the unit. Controlling at the corporate level could include EHS performance, or management audits of business units or subsidiaries. Lower-case *p*lanning, *o*rganizing, *s*taffing, *d*irecting, and *c*ontrolling activities involve weekly or daily work plans, reallocation of resources for different anticipated activities, routine replacement of staff, tracking quality, etc.

Behaviors of Individuals in Organizations

Expectations of Employee Performance

Theories on the expected behavior of employees in industrial settings vary dramatically. There appears to be more literature on this particular aspect of management then on any other single management issue. The range of variation can be demonstrated by examining two theories formulated by Douglas McGregor in 1960 from ideas developed by other management researchers.[47] McGregor labeled his theories, "Theory X" and "Theory Y."

Theory X holds that employees are naturally lazy, lack ambition, avoid responsibility, and are indifferent to the needs of the organization. Consequently, Theory X managers must motivate employees to behave in a manner that suits the needs of the organization. This involves leading the employees to each successive step in the process of their work, vigilantly monitoring employee performance, and continuously providing stimuli to keep employees productive and on-track.

Theory Y holds that work is an inherent human activity and if provided the right environment, employees voluntarily will work toward achieving organizational goals. The *right* work environment will encourage creative thought and empower employees. Enhanced self-esteem and personal sense of worth are the intangible rewards harvested by the individual involved in the right work environment. Thus, theory Y managers are concerned with developing and maintaining work situations that motivate employees by providing them with guided opportunities to satisfy their inherent self-actualization needs by contributing toward the organization's goals and objectives.

McGregor believed that Theory X was the prevalent model at play in the industry at that time.[48] He argued, however, that the reason this was so was not that employees lacked the inherent qualities predicted by Theory Y, but rather because the repressive organizational climate in industry teaches this self-defeating behavior.

An interesting parallel may be drawn between expectations regarding the employee's performance as it relates to the pursuit of organizational goals, and as it relates to the protection of the environment. If organizational culture can repress an employee's natural propensity to do good work, it may be capable of also subduing other such tendencies. It is easy to base an intuitive argument for an inherent human capacity for protection of the environment upon the observation that almost everyone values clean air, water, and soil. This argument is strengthened considerably when the connection is made between the basic human need for a life-supporting environment, and the well-documented impelling human predisposition toward survival.

Views of the Organization

The Behavioral Science Approach to Management

The behavioral science approach to management applies elements of individual and social psychology in order to understand, predict, and guide organizational behavior and performance. This approach developed within the field of human relations, which began in response to the results of a celebrated series of research activities conducted at a Western Electric plant during the late 1920s and early 1930s known as the *Hawthorne Studies*.[49]

Initially attempting to establish relationships between the employees' levels of production and variations in their physical working conditions, these studies revealed that social variables in the workplace are more significant, with respect to productivity, than physical variables.

Viewing the organization as a social system is central to understanding the behavioral science approach. Individual motivation, communication, and motivation-based leadership, are all key elements in this approach.

The Systems Approach to Management

The systems approach looks at the activities of the whole organization rather than focusing on those of individual units within the organization. In the broadest application, it can include both functional and social systems. However, while behavioral science research centers on understanding and developing motivational techniques, systems approach research focuses on improving decision-making methodologies and is often impersonal.[50]

The systems approach cuts across the five functions of management through information flow channels. As in the behavioral science approach, communication is a key element. It applies scientific methodology to the whole organization, similar to the way Frederick Taylor did to the organizational component. The study of this holistic approach is called *management science,* marking its similarities to, yet distinguishing it from, Taylor's narrower *scientific management.*

Philosophies of Management

An effective management philosophy provides the foundation upon which the organization is formed and decisions are made. In *Management in Action,* William D. Hitt identifies the following ten basic requirements for establishing an effective management philosophy.[51] The philosophy of management should:

1. be the foundation stone for the entire enterprise
2. include a clear statement of values
3. contain a clear statement of goals
4. contain a clear statement of strategies
5. be internally consistent
6. demonstrate an awareness of the larger environment
7. be operational

8. be internalized by all members of the management team
9. be communicated to all employees
10. be self-renewing

These insightful policy requisites recognize and support both behavioral science and systems approaches to management.

In a survey of 30 environmental, health and safety management professionals,[52] participants were asked to identify and prioritize the policy requirements that are most important for: (a) setting management objectives; (b) establishing and propagating the culture of an organization; and (c) achieving optimal organizational effectiveness. The results illuminate the perceived importance of the various elements.

Item 3, *a clear statement of goals,* Item 4, a *clear statement of strategies,* and Item 1, *the philosophy serves as the foundation of the enterprise,* were identified as the most important for setting management objectives. All other items were determined to be significantly less important. Embodied in the three selected items are a statement of what the organization hopes to achieve (4), how it intends to get there (2), and a verification that what is stated is in fact what the organization believes (1).

Item 2, a *clear statement of values,* and Item 8, *internalized beliefs,* were identified as having the highest priority with respect to establishing and propagating the organizational culture. Item 5, *internal consistency,* Item 7, *operational practice,* and Item 9, *communications,* followed closely behind. Here the top ranked requirements are those that identify what is important about what the organization does (2) and those that emphasize the need that stakeholders believe it (8). The second-tier elements represent the means of maintaining and strengthening these beliefs.

Item 9, *communications,* Item 10, *self-renewal,* and Item 3, *a clear statement of goals,* topped the list associated with overall effectiveness. Interestingly, all the other items were grouped close behind.Not surprisingly, the results suggest that as the scope expands from setting specific management objectives to achieving optimal organizational effectiveness, more and more of the management policy elements come into play.

Functions and Philosophies

While management functions define what the organization does in a very specific sense and how it does what it does, management philosophies define what the organization does in the broad sense, why it does what it does, and why it does what it does in the way it does. For example, a company that is concerned about market sensitivity to environmental issues may adopt the following policy:

> To do our part as a responsible corporate citizen to help protect the environment by only developing new products that are environmentally

> responsible and to ensure that.this is so through intensive internal research and appropriate external third-party verification.

Without citing specific details as to what must be done to develop a new product, this policy statement states that the company wants "to help protect the environment by only developing new products that are environmentally responsible" (defining what it wants to do in the broad sense), "to do our part as a responsible corporate citizen," (explaining why it wants to do this), and "ensure that this is so through intensive internal research and appropriate external third-party verification" (providing a strategy to accomplish this).

Corresponding functional approaches might be to modify product development procedures to include, define, and require environmental life-cycle-assessment and design-for-the-environment as necessary steps in the company's product development cycle, as well as to require all new products to be labeled for environmental friendliness by one or more recognized green-labeling organizations prior to commercialization. This specifically explains what will be done and describes how it will be done.

Variation and Consistency

An effective management policy helps explain variation within the organization. Internal consistency, identified as one of the policy requirements, does not imply functional consistency. While functional consistency may make sense among the business units or departments of an organization that are involved in similar activities under similar conditions, it is a point of fact that an organization involved in significantly diverse activities will justifiably have functional variations among its diverse business units or departments. For purposes of harmony and cooperation, it is important for members of the organization to understand the reasons for these differences.

Consistency with a corporate-wide philosophy goes a long way toward explaining, understanding, and justifying functional variation among units. For example, a company's environmental management policy may declare that the company will lead the industry in environmental performance in each of the countries in which it operates. If there are significant variations in the accepted environmental standards and practices in those countries, then it follows that the company's environmental management functions may vary from one location to another while it still maintains a leading position in all. The application of the policy remains consistent, and a stakeholder in one country can understand why his or her environmental management program is more or less rigorous than that in a similar operation in another company facility located somewhere else.

Functional variation may occur within an organization because different units are involved in different activities. Additionally, varying levels of environmental risk may be associated with the different activities. West and Michaud[53] provide an effective means of characterizing organizations by

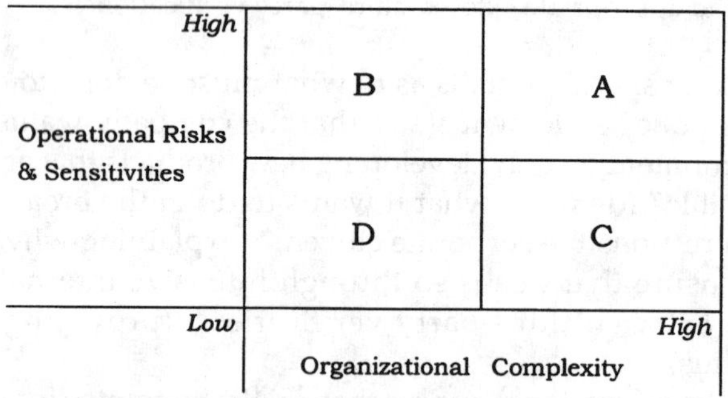

FIGURE 3-1
West & Michaud's Environmental, Health and Safety Program Matrix (From West, Gordon A., and Michaud, Ronald W., *Principles of Environmental, Health and Safety Management*, Government Institutes, 1995).

plotting their respective measures of organizational complexity and operational risk on a two-dimensional Environmental, Health, and Safety (EHS) Program matrix presented above:

- ❑ Organizations in Quadrant A have complex operations and high EHS risks. These may be international corporations with diversified and possibly unrelated product lines. They tend to be large, and business units may operate with considerable amounts of autonomy.
- ❑ Quadrant C companies are similar to those in Quadrant A, but with low EHS risks.
- ❑ Quadrant B and D companies are less complicated, with few or closely related product lines. They may be large or small. Control tends to be more centralized in these quadrants.
  - — Quadrant B companies have significant EHS risks.
  - — Quadrant D companies have small EHS risks.

The importance of philosophical and functional consistency for organizations in each of the quadrants can be examined as a function of complexity, by breaking the matrix into columns (B&D — low, and A&C — high), and as a function of risk, by breaking the matrix into rows (C&D — low, and B&A — high).

The varied nature of a complex organization will necessitate some functional variation. Consistent management philosophy in complex organizations is important because it justifies functional variation among business units and departments. Following this argument, the importance of functional consistency rates lower than philosophical consistency for quadrants

A&C. If, for the sake of comparison, the numerical values 0 and 1 are assigned respectively to represent low and high levels of importance, then for A and C, Functional consistency (Fc) = 0, and Philosophical consistency (Pc) = 1.

In low-complexity organizations (the extreme case being the small, domestic, single-product company), functional consistency is likely to be more important than in high-complexity organizations because a greater percentage of the organization is involved in the same activities. Philosophical consistency is less important simply because there is less functional variation. So for quadrants B and D, Fc = 1 and Pc = 0.

Considering only the EHS outcomes, not the overall productivity of the organization, it can be concluded that the lower the EHS risks, the less important optimum performance becomes. If there is little EHS risk associated with what an organization does, then no matter how inefficiently it is run, there will be no major adverse EHS outcomes. Conversely, high-EHS-risk organizations stand to suffer significant damages, and well thought-out and consistently applied management philosophy and functions take on a more important role. So, for low-risk organizations C&D, Fc = 0 and Pc = 0, and for high-risk operations A and B, Fc = 1 and Pc = 1.

Tallying the result of these two analyses produces the following table:

Quadrant	Importance of Functional Consistency	Importance of Philosophical Consistency
A	1 (MI)	2 (VI)
B	2 (VI)	1 (MI)
C	0 (LI)	1 (MI)
D	1 (MI)	0 (LI)

Note:: MI = Moderately Important; VI = Very Important; LI = Less Important.

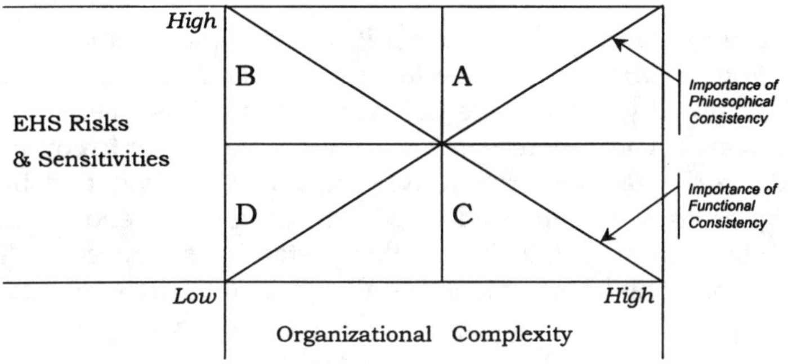

FIGURE 3-2
The importance of philosophical and functional management consistency as functions of environmental, health and safety risks, and organizational complexity.

Plotting these results on West and Michaud's EHS Program Matrix (Figure 3-2) reveals that the importance of functional consistency generally increases with an increase in risk, but is inversely proportional to organizational complexity. The importance of philosophical consistency increases as risk increases and as the organization becomes more complex.

Total Quality Management

Perusing the preceding paragraphs, it is easy to get the sense that management is an evolving science, each generation building upon previous experiences with increasing complexity and sophistication. Total quality management (TQM) is presented near the end of this chapter in correspondence to this chronology, but also to highlight its importance in current and developing environmental management strategies and as a component of voluntary environmental management.

Actually, TQM has its roots in the work done by W. Edwards Deming during World War II to help American manufacturers improve performance by applying statistical theory to production process control.[54] It was adopted very successfully by Japanese business as an operating philosophy after the war, and it reemerged in the west in the 1980s. TQM seeks to eliminate defects by continuously improving the overall process.

The Philosophy

Deming's philosophy of operation is built upon a set of principles that he calls the "14 Points."[55] While all are relevant to environmental management strategy, ten are central to the most current thought.

- *Create constancy of purpose toward improvement of product and service, with the aim to become competitive, stay in business, and provide jobs.* Traditionally, environmental management has been a reactive endeavor. The only reason to improve was in order to comply with regulatory requirements. Environmental objectives and business objectives were perceived to exist at the opposite ends of the possibilities balance. Current thinking establishes a specified level of environmental performance as a legitimate business objective.
- *Cease dependence on inspection to achieve quality. Eliminate the need for inspection on a mass basis by building quality into the product in the first place.* Inherent in a system that is dependent upon inspection for quality is the assumption that it is acceptable to produce some specified number of defective products. Remedial action is initiated only when this number is exceeded. Similarly, the traditional

environmental management strategy is founded upon the assumption that it is acceptable to produce waste. Consequently, the role of the environmental manager traditionally began at end of the discharge pipe. Here, Deming calls for an *upstream* investment of effort in order to eliminate defective products and process-wastes.

- *End the practice of awarding business on the basis of price tag. Instead, minimize total cost. Move toward a single supplier for any one item, on a long-term relationship of loyalty and trust.* This step creates external partners and, in essence, incorporates them into the organization. The objectives are to improve overall quality and reduce overall cost. The significant liabilities associated with improper waste disposal have already sensitized environmental managers to the importance of establishing relationships with responsible waste treatment, storage, and disposal facilities. Examples of new environmental initiatives focusing on suppliers and customers include: preferential procurement practices for environmentally responsible products, returnable packaging, product buy-back policies, and cooperative efforts to conserve resources and prevent pollution.
- *Improve constantly and forever the system of production and service, to improve quality and productivity, and thus constantly decrease costs.* This is the dynamic element of the Deming model. It rejects the notion that defects and waste are inevitable. From an environmental perspective, it compliments the move away from the *end-of-pipe* treatment and acknowledges the objective to reduce overall cost.
- *Institute training on the job.* In a dynamic organizational system, continuous training is a necessity. Policy changes without operational level training can create confusion and foster an apathetic view of leadership.
- *Institute leadership. The aim of supervision should be to help people and machines and gadgets to do a better job.* Philosophical change tends to require more leadership than does functional change. Employees need to assimilate the new reality of the workplace as well as its new procedures. New approaches to environmental management introduce dramatic philosophical change into the organization. This is especially so in functional units that traditionally have not had responsibility for protecting the environment.
- *Drive out fear, so that everyone may work effectively for the company.* By establishing mechanisms to identify deficiencies as part of the operational process, organizations can avoid the problem of mismanagement due to misinformation associated with workers being afraid to identify problems. By standing back far enough to view the larger organizational system over an extended period of time, it becomes possible to see how an incremental cost increase at the unit level may result in an overall decrease in cost for the

organization – thus the unit may be rewarded for an action that otherwise would have appeared inefficient or unnecessary.

- *Break down barriers between departments.* Internal communication and collaboration among departments are essential elements of quality improvement. This is so especially with respect to environmental management, which tends to exist in isolation from other business functions. While this tendency is often attributed to the prescriptive nature of environmental regulatory process, the more profound realization is that it results because environmental costs have not been internalized in these other business functions.
- *Eliminate numerical goals. Substitute leadership.* Numerical quotas typically lack adequate social relevance to serve as meaningful goals. And, while it might not be possible or advisable to eliminate the numerical requirements set forth in environmental regulations, it nonetheless is not a requirement that they be used to define the organization's environmental management goals. In fact, the preoccupation of regulatory agencies with numbers stands as a potential obstacle to developing an understanding of environmental issues and impacts. Environmental regulations do not specify how the environment is impacted by the types of releases they govern, nor how complying with a specified standard mitigates the impacts or benefits the environment. Taken in its entirety, TQM is about reaching for optimal performance. For the individual, in most cases, this requires more than a set of instructions. It requires comprehension of the larger relevance of each action, an understanding not conveyed by numbers alone.
- *Put everybody in the company to work to accomplish the transformation. The transformation is everybody's job.* Every task requires resource use. Every employee uses resources and participates in determining overall productivity and quality. To exclude anyone from the process of change and quality improvements is to guarantee that optimal performance will not be attained. Again, this has special meaning for environmental activities. Most individuals either have been excluded from environmental responsibilities or have had peripheral roles without any expectation that the relevance of their actions would be assimilated.

Principles of Total Quality Environmental Management

Deming's 14-point philosophy is embodied in four guiding principles of Total Quality Environmental Management.

- *Quality is defined by the stakeholders.* In the environmental arena an organization's list of stakeholders may include the customer, employee, regulator, neighbor, community, environmental advocacy groups, board of directors, financial and insuring institutions, potential business partners, and others. Stakeholders specify what is appropriate environmental quality for the organization.

- *Defects are eliminated at the source.* Waste is a defect. Eliminating waste at the source means that conservation of material, energy, and environmental resources become principal design criteria in developing or redeveloping products, services, and operations. The focus is on root causes of resource inefficiencies and the approach is to eliminate activities, materials, processes, etc. that do not add value.
- *Improvement is continuous.* For environmental managers this means that regulatory compliance becomes a part, rather than the entirety, of the operational motive. Results are measured and communicated in a continuous plan-do-check-act spiral of innovation and enhancements in which plans as well as processes are upgraded.
- *A cross-functional system's approach is taken.* Efforts are integrated across the organization. Environmental management teams are formed across departmental boundaries and represent the people, equipment, facilities, etc. involved in the various operations. The team addresses the quality requirements identified by the stakeholders.

Management Influences

Earlier in this chapter "management" was described as being composed of common managerial elements that are identifiable across a diversity of applications. These common elements are influenced, however, by the unique aspects of each diverse application. For example, in the field of information technology in 1998, managers need to factor in the workforce shortage of individuals with education or experience in the most current technological applications. This is a supply side issue for the staffing function, but clearly could have impacts on planning or organization functions as well. Marketplace economics predict that, barring external influence, the supply of information technologists will grow to meet the demand

External influences do exist, however, and may advance or retard the resolution of this discrepancy. Principal among non-marketplace influences is government regulation. For example, companies that work in the food services industry must factor in government standards and requirements governing food and health. Such influences are less likely to vary with the ebb-and-flow frequency of the marketplace. A list of generalizations about government regulations would be likely to mention their tendencies to build upon themselves, become more stringent with time, and overlap and contradict each other to the extent that compliance becomes a virtual impossibility. Additionally, decommissioning of regulations and laws is an infrequent occurrence, particularly when compared to the proliferation of new laws and the promulgation of new regulations. As a consequence, the total volume of government law and regulation continuously increases. Government influence over any activity can be expected at best to be static.

Public opinion is another external force that can influence an organization and its management. This force can extend well beyond consumer preferences based upon comparative price and quality of products. It may focus on a company's regard for its workers, for the communities in which it operates, and for the environment. At the international level, there may be industry- or activity-specific accords, protocols or voluntary standards that bear influence on an organization.

It is important to remember that it is people who manage and recognize that forces that influence an organization, influence the people who manage it. Environmental managers almost always are influenced by government, are frequently influenced by public opinion, and increasingly influenced by the marketplace and by international collaborations. Each of these influences will be discussed in greater depth in later chapters.

4

Defining Environmental Management

If you find a company that is environmentally responsible, the quality of management is such that ... they are most likely very good at everything they do.

*Ian Ihnatowycz**

Environmental Management System Model

Anyone who has taken out the garbage has done environmental management; managing waste is a fundamental part of environmental management. Moreover, if it is an individual's weekly responsibility to take out the garbage, then that person is part of an environmental management system. The environmental management system model illustrated in Figure 4-1 depicts other areas of responsibility that, depending upon the organization, may or may not be considered part of an environmental management system. Five major activity categories are identified in this model: Environmental Protection, Occupational Health & Safety, Environmental Program Management, Contractor Operations, and Product Stewardship.

It should be noted that responsibility for occupational health and safety may, and often does, exist as a separate system or systems within the organization, or as a parent system in which environmental protection is a component subsystem. Increasingly, however, organizations are combining their resources for managing environmental, health and safety aspects.

The various components may be included or excluded by design, i.e., as part of a plan consciously established at the organizational level in accordance with its environmental vision or policy, or by default as the result of the lack of a plan or design. Responsibilities may overlap or be duplicated among the various activity categories. For example, activities directed at pollution prevention may be identified as specific elements of good product stewardship, as part of an organization's overall efforts to protect the environment, and as a demonstrated commitment to protect its workers.

* Ihnatowycz, Ian. Quoted in *Business Strategy for Sustainable Development*. International Institute for Sustainable Development, 1992:10.

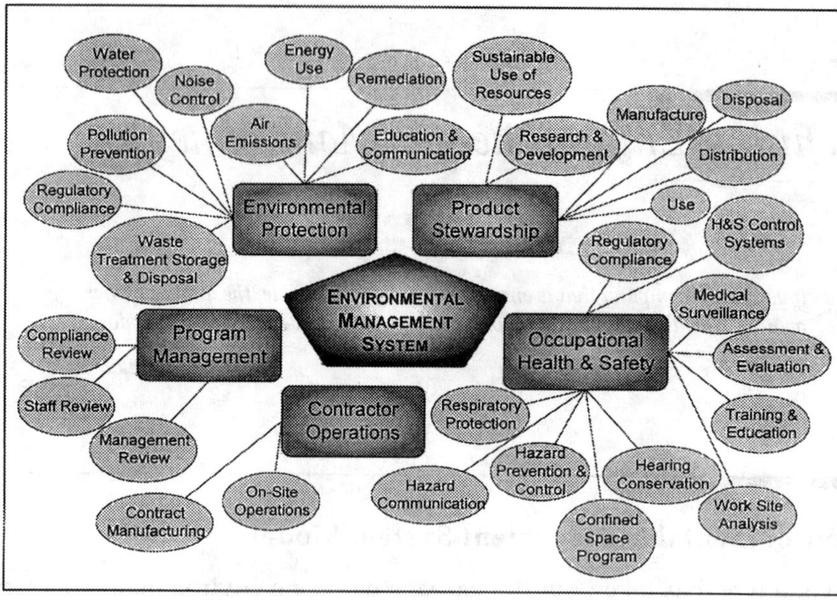

FIGURE 4-1
An Environmental Management System Model.

Environmental Protection

Almost every activity uses resources and has impacts on the environment. Some of these environmental impacts are regulated by government; most are not. Traditionally, the efforts of environmental managers have been directed at regulated activities only. In the broad universe of environmental affairs, this particular area of endeavor is labeled *environmental quality management* and is concerned principally with the control of discharges of specified wastes under specified circumstances to air, water, and land resources. Remediation of environmental problems associated with past practices also may demand much of the environmental manager's time. Natural resource usage typically has not been a major concern of environmental managers — the underlying operating principle regarding resource use is that economic forces will control its waste.

A close look at the activities of an environmental manager reveals that compliance with environmental laws and regulations occupies the predominant portion of his or her time. The implicit assumption has been that compliance with environmental regulations will result in environmental protection.

Fines, fees, penalties, and assessments associated with regulatory violations provide economic drivers for compliance. In addition, the rapid escalation throughout the 1980s of waste transport, treatment, and disposal fees produced economic incentives for companies to reduce the toxicity and quantity of their wastes. Recently, some of the more progressive organizations have expanded traditional perspectives to encompass all of their environmental aspects, regulated or not. Any efforts devoted to environmental protection beyond minimum state and federal mandates are voluntary efforts, and an organization that chooses to address its non-mandated environmental aspects is practicing voluntary environmental management.

Occupational Health and Safety

Occupational health and safety disciplines work together well. Safety is concerned most with immediate threats to employees, health with longer-term and chronic problems. Safety, health, and environment can be viewed as a sequential set of concerns that increase in scope in progression from the individual to the outside world.[56] Like with environmental management, health and safety management programs are very concerned with regulatory compliance. However, beyond the mandated drivers exist very significant economic incentives for improved health and safety performance. These are associated with the potential to reduce lost time due to injury or illness, reduce insurance fees and liabilities, improve morale, and increase productivity. Traditionally, environmental managers have been concerned with only the health and safety aspects associated with traditional environmental management activities like contaminated site investigation, spill response, and waste handling, storage, treatment, transport, and disposal.

Environmental Program Management

Management of the environmental program or department itself is an element of the overall EMS. Responsibilities typically include: staff development and deployment, assessing environmental quality status with respect to regulatory compliance and conformance with company standards, identifying applicable regulatory mandates, securing and tracking appropriate permits, tracking wastes and allocating environmental costs, securing necessary resources, and managing operational budgets.

Traditionally, both environmental activities and environmental managers remained in the periphery of the main business of the organization — at the end-of-the-pipe, so to speak. Increasingly, however, organizations are delegating environmental responsibilities to their non-environmental managers. Of the multitude of environmental activities presented in Figure 4-1, many will not be in the hands of the professional environmental management staff. Rather, the environmental management department may be called upon by a production line manager to help reduce environment-related costs in that unit. The responsibility for implementing and continuing to operate the recommended solutions may reside with the production manager.

The rapidly evolving world of information technology provides a good analogy for explaining this shared responsibility. At one point in time, data processing occurred only in data processing centers run by data processing experts. Now, data processing occurs on everyone's desk and today's data processing experts (i.e., the information technologists) serve the organization by helping it identify and install the right hardware, software, networks, etc., and by helping individual units with unit-specific needs. Similarly, a large part of the responsibilities of tomorrow's environmental manager will be to provide the support that each business unit needs to define and manage its environmental aspects, and to ensure that the organization has the resources it needs to conform to its environmental policies and meet the goals and objectives it sets.

Contractor Operations

Since Allied Chemical's Kepone incident in James River, Virginia,* businesses have been concerned about environmental liabilities that may be incurred as a result of actions taken by their contractors. Environmental responsibility tends to remain with the parent organization. Also, voluntary environmental management commitments easily may extend beyond issues of liability to include those associated with self-specified levels of environmental performance. Organizations will decide the boundaries of their voluntary efforts. Organizational commitments to worker health and safety may result in specified levels of health and safety related performance from contractors.

Product Stewardship

From an environmental perspective, comprehensive product stewardship involves minimizing adverse impacts on material, energy, and environmental resources in each step along the life-cycle continuum from extraction of raw materials (e.g., ores, timber, petroleum, etc.), to production of those materials into useful building blocks (e.g., bars, boards, energy products, etc.), to conversion into goods (i.e., manufacturing), to distribution, to consumption, and ultimately to disposal. If this continuum is viewed as a flow of materials through the economy, then good product stewardship will retard the flow from the extraction stage to the disposal stage by increasing design life, reusing materials, reducing waste, etc. It will minimize energy use and adverse impacts on the environment at each step along the way.

From occupational health and safety perspectives, product stewardship involves minimizing adverse impacts on the health and safety of the employees involved in each step along the continuum. Occupational health and safety concerns are sometimes intertwined with product safety aspects of product stewardship, which focuses on the related health and safety of distributors and end users.

---

* See *Assuming Responsibility* under the section entitled **Environmental Management Circa 1980** in Chapter 2 of this book.

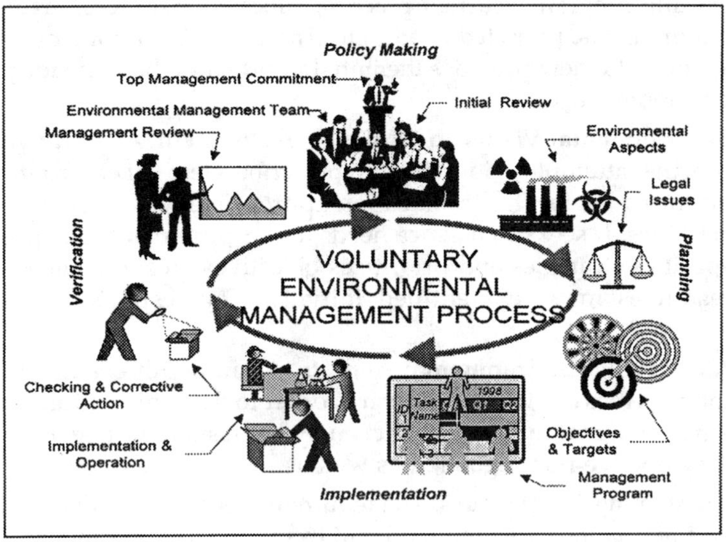

FIGURE 4-2
The Voluntary Environmental Management Process.

Voluntary Environmental Management

Since there are no regulations to guide voluntary environmental management efforts, the organization must pro-actively identify the non-regulated environmental aspects of its activities, determine which are significant, and which it will address. Since such a commitment requires resources and widespread cooperation, voluntary environmental management programs typically require top-level support. Voluntary environmental management thus tends to be a strategic, cross-functional process by which an organization identifies and achieves its necessary and appropriate short- and long-term environmental performance goals. A voluntary environmental management process model is depicted in Figure 4-2.

Environmental Management Systems

The Environmental Management System (EMS) is a component of the organization's overall management system. Generally, it involves four categories of activities: Policy Making, Planning, Implementation and Verification. Specific activities in this continuum may include:

- ❑ **An Initial Environmental Management Review.** This involves gathering information on related performance history, current concerns, existing programs, current practice, allocated resources, regulatory requirements, projected needs, etc. The Initial Environmental Management Review provides the initial information baseline for policy development.

- **Environmental Vision and Policy Development.** An iterative process that attempts to identify and prescribe a level of environmental performance for the organization appropriate to its functions and activities. It seeks to balance needs and aspirations against cost. It specifies strategies and prioritizes objectives. Resource needs and resources may be identified initially. Key responsibilities are assigned.
- **Identifying Environmental Aspects.** An in-depth examination of the activities of the organization in order to determine all associated environmental impacts. Impacts may be positive or negative. This may involve non-regulated as well as regulated activities.
- **Identifying Legal Issues.** The requirements of environmental laws and regulations are identified and examined. Depending upon the organization and its environmental vision and policies, voluntary standards and guidelines may be included in this activity. Such standards may be set forth in international agreements or accords, by professional organizations, or by government.
- **Planning Activities.** Environmental management goals and strategies established in the organization's policy need to be translated into action plans for managing its environmental aspects in accordance with prioritized objectives. Thresholds for action may be determined during planning steps. Methods of measuring and evaluating performance are decided and contingency plans developed. Resource needs and sources will be determined more closely. Responsibility is assigned at operational levels.
- **Resource Allocations.** Organizational resources are redistributed and units may be restructured to correspond with action plans.
- **Setting Objectives and Targets.** Programmatic or unit-specific objectives and targets are established for the next year or reporting period.
- **Establishing Practices and Procedures.** Environmental management approaches are developed, refined, and successes are shared among units with similar operations.
- **Implementation.** The detailed and documented plan is put into action across the organization. Employees are trained, programs are initiated, performance is tested, and adjustments are made during an initial shake-down period.
- **Monitoring and Corrective Action.** Once the plan is underway, performance is measured and adjustments made as necessary.
- **Management Review.** Periodically, the management team reviews the performance reports and evaluates the extent to which intended

goals and objectives are being met. Discrepancies may warrant modifications to the plan, resource reallocations, personnel changes, or reassessment of the expectations.

- **Continuous Improvement.** As objectives are met, priorities may change and higher plateaus may come within reach. Management may choose to broaden the scope of its environmental vision or elevate its goals.

Do What You Say!

Statements of goals and objectives are essential to the planning process and to the operation of any environmental management system. But stated goals and objectives without corresponding achievements can do more harm than good. Organizations today must do what they say they do. Toward this end, an EMS will do two things for the organization:

1. It will provide the means of developing and implementing an appropriate environmental policy.
2. It will provide the means to determine the extent to which the policy is being implemented.

A Matter Of Perspective

By its very nature, the EMS is a strategic component of business management. Consistent with the TQM approach and with good common sense, if you stand back far enough to view the whole picture, you will see more clearly how the pieces fit. Designing an organization-wide EMS provides this perspective. Implementing it polishes and fine-tunes the organization's environmental understanding.

Continual improvement is the process of improving performance to move an organization towards its environmental policy goals. While at first it may look more like corrective action, it is much more than that. When changes in practices are made for the purpose of moving toward identified objectives or targets, they are corrective actions. When changes are made to the objectives or targets to move the organization closer to its EHS policy goals, it is continuous improvement. Continual improvement magnifies environmental focus and expands environmental opportunities. It moves an organization to a point where it can enhance its policy goals.

A good EMS drives an organization towards activities and provides it with capabilities that are of interest to its stakeholders. An EMS will help the organization focus on pollution prevention and diminish the need for corrective action, achieve levels of environmental performance appropriate for the nature, scale, and impacts of its activities, products and services, achieve and maintain regulatory compliance, and improve continuously.

Some stakeholders may give preference to, or require evidence of, good environmental performance from supplier organizations or, in some cases, customers. A good EMS provides this evidence. In addition, certain governmental programs (regulatory and voluntary) may give preference to, or require such performance from, organizations under their jurisdictions or otherwise eligible for their programs.

More than the Sum of Its Parts

Voluntary environmental management is more than the sum of the organization's regulatory requirements. It is concerned with economic and environmental risks, and seeks the most effective mix of technological applications and management strategies to minimize both. Short-term environmental goals sought by most environmental managers include regulatory compliance and avoided costs. Long-term goals include increased efficiency and competitiveness. Taken to its logical, but not always obvious, long-term conclusion, voluntary environmental management will merge with strategic economic management, converging at the point of sustainability.

Section II

A Case for Voluntary Environmental Management

Note: This section and the one that follows contains numerous quotations of and references to environmental professionals interviewed during this work. These individuals are categorized by their professional affiliations and identified by the category codes listed below. The codes will appear in parentheses as references or following specific quotes.

- **(EPA):** Environmental Protection Agency Official
- **(SG):** State Government Official
- **(IEM):** Industrial Environmental Manager
- **(NGO):** Non-Governmental Environmental Advocacy Organization Representative
- **(ISO):** ISO 14000 Development Team Member

5

The National System of Environmental Standards

A Non-Uniform System

Environmental professionals generally agree that a national system of environmental standards now exists in the United States, particularly in contrast to the situation as it existed in the early 1970s. Most do not believe, however, that the system is 'uniform' or that it is uniformly applied: "If you go media-by-media, chemical-by-chemical, it's different from state-to-state, federal-to-state, local-to-state, local-to-federal" (SG). The variation is not inherent in the federal system which "provides a floor that's uniform" (EPA), but is introduced at the state and local level. Variation exists because of a wide range of historical, economic, and political issues. For example, regarding a state's environmental programs, a governor may decide that, "he or she wants to say, 'This is the first in the nation; this is the best in the nation; this is the strongest in the nation'" (NGO). In order to do that, the state must require more stringent control than does the federal government. Such state-to-state variations in regulatory standards, or in the interpretation of regulatory standards, are often accompanied by variation in regulatory agency infrastructures, and thus moving from location to location impacts not only what can be done, but also the path taken to get there.

Strong concerns exist about the large number of environmental regulations, their labyrinthine structure and organization, and their numerous instances of overlapping authority and contradictory demands. Moreover, they are inconsistent, "with some areas extremely heavily regulated and other areas not at all touched ... [creating] isolated areas of goals and objectives for ... companies to reach ... but no holistic approach" (NGO). Perhaps the most frustrating issue of all is that "you can't comply with everything 100% the way [environmental regulatory law] is written right now" (EPA).

A Focus on Compliance, Not Protection

The very specific nature of some environmental laws and regulations tend to perpetuate growth of more of the same with the consequence that valid decisions made concerning one rule often overlap others that make no sense when considered in their context. This is illustrated in the example that follows involving the handling of waste isopropyl alcohol at an IBM facility:

- An aqueous waste at an IBM facility containing a 24 percent concentration of isopropyl alcohol is considered hazardous under one regulatory rule because it is flammable.
- Under another rule, thermal destruction at 99.9999 percent efficiency is identified as the 'best practice' for treating flammable waste.
- A third rule allows alternative treatment, but only if it is equivalent to 'best practice.'
- IBM has an on-site liquid waste treatment facility capable of treating this particular waste in a manner that all parties agree will afford adequate protection for the environment, but since it is only 99 percent effective, it is not allowed.
- As a consequence IBM must incur the cost of shipping and have it treated it off-site.

The three rules taken in combination prohibit IBM from sending this waste to its own on-site treatment facility which is perfectly capable of treating it. This problem has less to do with protecting the environment than it does with complying with specific rules written for other circumstances. It is an institutional problem. While it is probable that situations like this eventually can be resolved, the "resolution likely will result in another specific rule which down the road can create a problem for yet another situation" (EPA). According to EPA,[57] what actually did happen in this case was that IBM submitted a Project XL proposal to EPA to allow it to treat this waste in its wastewater on-site treatment plant. Then a number of stakeholder meetings were held to develop the proposed project. The XL proposal was withdrawn, however, when permission to treat the waste at the on-site plant was granted by EPA to IBM under a "Determination of Equivalent Treatment" provision. EPA identifies this as a project that was "Successfully Facilitated by XL."[58] The celebratory nature of this accomplishment is diminished by the magnitude of the effort required to make a decision about what was an obvious solution. In addition, the Project XL program, heralded as the flagship of regulatory reform, has been criticized for selecting projects, including this one, that focus on getting existing rules to work rather than on innovation and developing new strategies for the 21st century in accordance with the objectives of that program.

> If you look at 13 or 14 [XL] projects that EPA has endorsed, I dare say nine or ten of those are really regulatory relief. They are really *not* excellence in leadership, they're really more regulatory relief because the current structure won't allow it to happen (SG).

The IBM example reveals a fundamental problem with the implementation of environmental laws and regulations: *it focuses on compliance, rather than on protecting the environment*. The example also suggests that economic sensibility is not a major consideration in environmental regulatory decision-making.

Interpreting Guidelines as Gospel

Confusing and inconsistent application of law and regulations is exacerbated by agencies that treat governmental guidelines and guidance documents as if they were law. Guidance, or interim policies, may be developed by agencies as interim stopgap measures for situations encountered, but for which regulation has not yet been adopted. In such cases, an agency may insist that permit applicants subscribe to the standards set forth in the guidance rather than to those established in existing law or regulation. Historically this has been a cause of disagreement between regulators and the regulated. The principal area of contention involves the difficulty faced by a regulated organization in attempting to plan future activities without being able to predict what will be expected of it.

Other guidance policies are not intended as precursors to new mandates, but are provided by the agency simply as a set of higher standards for those who would use them. Frustration arises when an agency leverages its authority to force constituents to adhere to a higher set of otherwise non-mandated standards. Challenges to such abuse are relatively few for fear of reprisal.

> This is a classic case where the federal government puts out guidelines. Their guidelines are not, in fact, regulatory, statutory guidelines [i.e., mandates], but some states interpret them as [such] … and impose those numbers verbatim and other states don't do that. So this creates chasms between the state programs where it might be a lot more beneficial to be operating in one state vs. another based on some of the regulatory requirements or lack of the regulatory requirements (IEM).

Consistency of interpretation is a basic tenet of law. The variety of interpretations and uses of guidance documents detract from the quality of environmental regulatory law and adds to the patchwork characteristic of its implementation.

Lousy Science and Not Enough of It

Challenges to the quality of the science, and skepticism regarding the extent of its use in environmental regulatory decision-making, threaten the likelihood of increased partnership between industry and government. Concerns about the quality of science center on the charge that regulatory decisions are based on the results of risk models that are unrealistically over-conservative and which become more so over time. This "tends to work against the notion that standards and regulations are reasonable and rational and [that] there's a good place for them" (IEM).

Skepticism about the use of science is based on the fact that on occasion, environmental managers with multiple-site responsibilities must contend with political influence (i.e., elected and otherwise) as a principal consideration for environmental decision-making in one or more of the jurisdictions in which they operate.

> It might be nice to say that it is all based on science and technical and it's very logical, but in fact it's not. Some of it may be there. But there is a heavy dose of politics that gets involved too … And, if you don't take that into account, and you don't realize that that's what's going on, you're going to get blindsided (IEM).

Concerns about the validity of environmental regulatory decision-making lead to frustrations, and detriments efforts to encourage partnerships among the various stakeholder groups as do the problems of uniformity, purpose and consistency, discussed in the preceding sections.

A Faulty Vision

Generally, it is accepted that "the 26 years that EPA has been around has … forced a lot of culture change and it's forced a lot of compliance" (SG). The social reality in most large U.S. companies today is that compliance with environmental regulatory law *is* part of doing business. Yet some question the appropriateness of that culture change and suggest that perhaps our decision-makers were not looking far enough into the future when they conceived the current regulatory system.

> As a culture, we have just assumed that industry or business, or commerce can pollute, and we've set up for 40 years, laws that said, 'okay, you can pollute [i.e., generate wastes], but once you do, you need to clean up to these standards [i.e., before discharging it to the environment].' Everything is geared to it: legislation, the regulation, the public's mindset, businesses' mindset, most regulators' mindsets (SG).

Perhaps it is time for the nation to examine its long-term goals and identify the destination at which it wishes to eventually arrive.

Adequacy of the Nation's Environmental Standards for Use as Private-Sector Environmental Management Targets

Beyond the question of whether air, water, and land quality standards present reasonable targets with respect to the ability of environmental managers to achieve them, is a larger issue of whether or not the current system for specifying and achieving those standards, taken as a whole, is adequate and appropriate at this time and the move into the 21st century. The existing system is criticized as "a one-size-fits-all approach ... that doesn't work anymore" (SG). The generic approach applicable 25 years ago, when dealing with end-of-pipe discharges, becomes increasingly inappropriate as the focus of environmental efforts moves *upstream* in the production process from the end-of-pipe discharge, to the production floor, and ultimately to the offices in which products and services are designed, and where decisions regarding whether to offer them are made.

The general assessments of the adequacy of the nation's system of environmental regulatory law and enforcement range from moderately critical to the extreme: "Everybody, including the agencies, realize that our legislative package is so out of whack .... anybody in their right mind would question the environmental saneness of that type of a system" (EPA). Overlapping, poorly aligned, and conflicting authorities give the impression that no relationship exists between one environmental medium and another. "The Clean Air Act really is not written to take water into consideration and vice versa and those two [Clean Air Act & Clean Water Act] don't necessarily care a whole heck of a lot about solid waste" (EPA). Consequently, a company working on cleaning up a significant problem in one medium may well be creating a problem in another. The U.S. system of environmental standards is viewed analogously as a collection of regulatory silos operating independently from each other which "don't take a good look at what's the best overall way to spend your money (IEM)."

Command-and-Control Inefficiencies

Command-and-control, enforcement-based, environmental regulatory strategy, employed to the extent that it is in the U.S., is an obstacle to getting U.S. organizations to pay more attention to the development of voluntary international environmental management standards as well as forces inefficiencies into the production system.

> Only in the U.S. do I run into resistance to international standards. Everywhere else in the world the attitude is let's see what it is about. Part of this, I think, is our conditioned response to operating in a command-and-control environment. People are used to not doing things unless they're told they have to. This is because they are told so much to do (ISO).

Command-and-control approaches interfere with an industry's ability to conduct its business efficiently because it discounts the value and often precludes the use of an industry's expertise in its respective areas of endeavor. Ironically, large progressive industry includes environmental protection as a legitimate component of doing business. Industry sees the problem as, "government telling industry, not only 'here's the standard that we want you to achieve, but here is how you have to achieve it.' So American industry is not able to engineer its own solutions to get to a particular objective" (ISO).

Government is aware of this criticism and generally accepts it as valid. As one EPA official noted, "we have, in many ways, eliminated or reduced risks from the glaring environmental problems that we identified 25 years ago ... problems are far more difficult to solve when you're at the margins" (EPA).

Even among organizations with traditions of strong command-and-control orientation, there is recognition that the current system is less than adequate. According to an NGO administrator:

> The reason ... the system is inefficient is that it consists of regulatory bureaucrats ... determining, at the margin, [and] in some cases far more deeply, how companies will run their business. Nobody would argue, I don't think, that that's not wrong ... the idea that some desk jockey who is an environmental engineer or scientist or a lawyer of some sort, can tell a plant manager how best to produce paper cups. It just doesn't make any sense. But that's what the regulations, by and large, say to do. So it's inefficient from the company's perspective because you've got somebody who doesn't care and doesn't understand your business, telling you how to run it (NGO).

The adequacy and appropriateness of the current system of environmental regulation are challenged as focus shifts from the end-of-the-pipe to the production floor, and as the level of pollution shifts from gross to subtle. Especially problematic are the implementation methodologies. Clearly, current environmental protection needs have become much more sophisticated than the tools that are in place to manage them.

6

A Quarter Century of Progress

Pendulum of Change

Many organizations that ignored the environmental aspects of their activities in the 1970s are overwhelmed by the attention that must be paid to them today. The "tyranny of legislation and regulations [make it] almost a full time job keeping track of what comes out of the various regulatory agencies on an ongoing basis" (IEM). Much has changed over the last quarter century regarding awareness of environmental concerns and allocation of environmental responsibility. "Most important is that in 1969 ... there was no reason whatsoever for the manager of a plant or the CEO of a business to ask an environmental question, much less answer it. Today there is" (NGO).

Today, top administrators and environmental managers in regulated organizations are aware of an environmental enforcement presence and have personal knowledge of instances in which companies and individuals were caught and punished for violating environmental regulations. They are also aware of companies that have gone out of business as a result of environmental liabilities. They deal on a daily basis with the substantial cost of compliance, and they work within an environmental management infrastructure that has resources and the authority to influence the activities of other departments and operations. Finally, they are acknowledged as legitimate professionals within their respective organizations. None of this was true in 1970.

Painful Metamorphosis

A consensus of opinion exists across all sectors of society that, in retrospect, the command-and-control structure was necessary 25 years ago in order to get industry to curtail its gross release of pollutants into the environment. It was "like hitting a horse with a two-by-four to get its attention" (SG). The approach was intentionally strong and confrontational: "It was important for Congress and the states to send a message that strong, swift, and certain enforcement was the way to go" (SG). The process was not open to a lot of debate or negotiation: "Starting from scratch, the thing was, 'just put the system in damn-it! And if you don't, we're going to kick you in the teeth'" (EPA).

At a minimum, the result is that industry no longer ignores the environmental aspects of its activities.

> For most companies, certainly the ones that have been touched by the hand of an enforcement agency but others [too] who are aware of what can happen, it has become far more financially viable to deal with environmental issues on their own pace, according to their own planning rather than having it being done in the context of an enforcement action where not only do they have to do the act, do the environmental control anyway, but they also have to pay a fine, [and] be found to have been a violator (EPA).

No Longer an Incidental Cost or Insignificant Benefit

The major portion of the costs associated with environmental management include those associated with proper disposal, permit fees, waste generator assessments, penalties, and remediation of waste sites. With few exceptions, little argument is offered regarding the appropriateness of these costs. Also, there is considerable awareness of the financial liability associated with improper disposal. The exception is in the area of remediation where the extremely high cost of cleanup is a direct result of very specific regulatory strategy governing how remedial investigations must be conducted.

Several factors have made companies aware of their environmental costs. First, companies had to meet the costs of complying with environmental regulations.

> The laws that were put on the books the last 25, 30 years, brought to manager's attention just how expensive it is, that this isn't anything that they could ignore anymore ... If you didn't have the 'regs' on the books and you didn't still have the enforcement hammer in the toolbox, I don't think you could use any other tools to get companies to look at things differently and look at their operations (SG).

Secondly, awareness was increased when it was recognized that the magnitude of the cost of environmental compliance was such that no longer could it be considered an incidental cost of doing business. This enlightenment was hastened for many companies in the late 1980s by the influence of the increasingly popular strategies of Total Quality Management.

> I think that what happened in the 80s, and maybe it began in the 70s, with total quality management taking hold, is that waste became lost profits. And one of the biggest areas of waste, if you consider the wasted money of treatment, disposal, potential liability, having to hire people to do reporting, having to file for permits, having to slow down your technology

> revolutions to keep up with the marketplace — that's waste! And so companies began to realize that some of the biggest places where they had waste was in the environmental arena. They've never tracked those cost before (SG).

Thirdly, there have been instances where a company's poor environmental performance led not only to its product no longer being considered the product of choice, but to an outright economic attack on the company. In 1971, industry was not very concerned about the ability of environmental activists to significantly impact its business. However:

> Now it has a big effect, because they can bring a lot of bad press, they can boycott products, they can send a message. They're very well organized, these environmental groups nationally, and they can impact the company (SG).

Amplifying these impacts, companies became aware of an increasing body of evidence that showed "that consumers would rather deal with companies that are perceived to be green companies than with others ..." (IEM). This provided an incentive for organizations to move toward environmentally 'friendly' products and practices.

Finally, a seed for economic sustainability may have been planted during the ongoing process of learning to internalize environmental costs. "The last 25 years have been critically important to have companies begin to understand [that] they have to a large extent, gotten a free ride by using irreplaceable raw materials" (SG).

Awareness, Knowledge, Procedures, and Protocols

With respect to its usage regarding environmental affairs, the word 'awareness' most often has to do with the public's interest in knowing about what was going on in the environment. In the early 1970s there was considerable environmental 'awareness' but very limited environmental knowledge (i.e., the information needed to make decisions about appropriate levels of environmental protection). "Nobody had ever been there before. That's where the uncertainty was. But it was clear that ... industry wasn't quite sure what to do ..." (SG). Over the past 25 years, the body of knowledge has expanded immensely and the levels of sensitivity of pollution detection equipment increased from parts-per-thousand to, for some compounds, parts-per-trillion — *a nine order of magnitude increase!*

> A lot of the Superfund sites that are being cleaned up now, became Superfund sites in the 50s, 60s and 70s perfectly legally, absolutely doing things that people thought were safe, effective, okay to do at that point in time. We've learned more about toxicology, about the migration of chemicals. We just know more (ISO).

Along with the increase in knowledge came the establishment of standardized procedures and protocols for managing those environmental aspects of an organization's activities covered by regulatory law. This relates directly to the question of whether or not there is now a system of environmental quality standards adequate for industry to take on more responsibility for protecting the environment. Such protocols most commonly were developed by government and were ensconced in its laws and regulations. For the most part, they are based on very conservative and overlapping assumptions of risk that tend to compound and magnify the built-in margins of safety. As such, they provide also a menu of generally accepted measures that can serve as the conservative end of a procedural spectrum for evaluating and managing environmental aspects either not covered by regulatory law, or to an extent that surpasses regulatory requirement.

Cultural Changes in Industry and Government

In the 1970s, industry's principal environmental concerns were the costs of putting in environmental control technologies and inequitable treatment under environmental law and regulation. The logic was simple: environmental costs, within reason, could be passed directly on to the consumer, but only if all producers of competing products or services were subject to the same requirements. Inequities among states' environmental programs, and even among regions within states, caused conflict and friction between industry and government. Government's imposition of an inequitable regulatory process was inconsistent with the tenets of a free-market business culture. By comparison, air emissions trading* today, controversial though it may be, provides incentives for environmental enhancements that make sense to business. Interestingly, this observation was made in 1970 by Herbert D. Doan, President of Dow Chemical, who explained that industry functions on a profit basis, and stated that it is incorrect to believe that industry will solve any problems without a customer for that solution.[59] He suggested that if a market in environmental control could be defined, then the marketplace would automatically take care of that need.

In the U.S., environmental management has evolved over the last quarter of a century to become a legitimate business practice and responsibility. "People are more aware. You see the fact that [good environmental management] makes sense to do" (SG). Concurrent with private-sector's acceptance of environmental management as a business function, evolved its common interest in doing things better and more efficiently.

> There is an acceptance by industry of the fact that they do have responsibility ... and maybe now there are more people who are willing

---

* *Note:* In air emissions trading, a regulated organization receives marketable credits for performance beyond that required by a permit to emit pollution to the atmosphere.

> to say, 'I can do a better job of this business wise – more effectively, more efficiently, if I can do it myself, than if government tells me how to do it (ISO).

Today, companies increasingly are becoming involved in a global 'playing field' that contains some gross inequities. Obviously, U.S. government is limited in its ability to level the world market. Some hope exists, however, that through international standards and cooperation, some movement can be made in this direction and that:

> ... through 14000 and some other vehicles, that we can see a lessening of the command-and-control framework [in the U.S.] and that other countries will come up and have a little more infrastructure than they have, so globally, the playing field is leveled a little bit. I think that we'll always be, as a most affluent society, able to clean things up a little better, protect our people a little better, learn a little bit more about the impacts. I think we'll always be on the leading edge so we'll always have costs to our society of doing that. That will have global impact but I think that it could be equalized quite a bit (ISO).

Where an abundance of evidence supports the case that a significant cultural change has occurred in industry and that it is an ongoing process, reports on changes in government have a more tentative flavor. Government is described as needing to change, or being ready to change, or trying to change. Common to such descriptions is the charge that the outmoded command-and-control structure still predominates.

> Twenty-five years later, now it's time to start looking in a different arena ... Should we now continue to say, 'This baseline which everybody is going to revolve around is got to be that everybody is going to cheat, so therefore let's whack the hell out of everybody' ... or should we now start saying, 'Let's start rewarding those that, in fact on their own volition, do things that are environmentally friendly and make good economic sense, and let's reserve our traditional strong enforcement and strong deterrents to those who don't want to or are unable or unwilling to comply with what society is mandating' (SG).

7

Reinventing Environmental Regulation in the U.S.

A Call for Change

Bruce Yandle, Alumni Professor at Clemson University and Senior Associate at the Perc Center for Policy and Legal Studies, speaks to the fact that in 1970 based on a very limited core of information, we created a command-and-control structure-based policy to deal with the environmental problems we were facing then, and that now it is time to use the information that has been compiled since to replace the 1970 centralized model with something that fits a world calling for flexibility, decentralization, and improved environmental protection.[60] He introduces two very broad approaches to regulating collective behavior:

1. The *systems* approach in which we seek to understand minute features of the problem, develop detailed rules of behavior covering every conceivable situation and then enforce those rules. The *systems* focus is on inputs, behavior, and technology, and produces command-and-control regulations. The assumption is that if the inputs are right, the outcomes will take care of themselves and while it is a rigid, rule-filled approach, it works pretty well for static and homogenous situations.
2. The *process* approach which develops constraints and linkages to the outcomes, but causes individual decision makers to account for their actions. The focus here is on outcomes, not on inputs.

Yandle criticizes the systems approach for focusing too much on inputs, often with the result that outcomes are relegated to the backseat. He talks about situations where air quality regulators will not consider water pollution problems, and how hazardous waste regulators are not allowed to make comparative assessments of priority sites or to vary their allocation of efforts. He says the one-size-fits-all approach does not work well for a diverse and rapidly changing industrial economy.

According to George S. Hawkins, Esq., Senior Advisor, EPA Region I, we need new environmental protection initiatives today because the existing environmental regulatory structure represents an outdated response to 25-year-old needs.[61] Ironically, efforts early on in the Clinton administration to reinvent environmental management were derailed by the all-out assault of the 104th Congress on the EPA. While the President stood firm, and with strong public support routed the Republican offensive, the wedge between those who would call for increased command-and-control regulation and those who want regulatory reform was driven deeper. Running the risk of being identified with the more crude and mean spirited efforts of the 104th Congress, Hawkins says that EPA can and should change. He said that such risk is the consequence of a just vanquished assault.

In his white-paper, "The Eagle Agenda: An Agenda for the Future of Environmental Protection," Hawkins explained that our system of environmental protection exists as a response to the tremendous increase in industrial production which grew from an index of 22.7 in 1947, to 121.9 in 1995, with 1987 having an index of 100, serving as the basis for this comparison.[62] This represents a 527 percent increase. Stimulated by a burning river in Cleveland, buried toxins in Love Canal, and an American public demanding environmental protection, officials responded by creating laws and the EPA. The method was simple and straightforward: Congress identified risks to air, water, and land, and identified the major source of risk to be end-of-the-pipe discharges, primarily coming from industry; Congress then empowered the EPA and charged it to reduce point source discharges.

Negotiation was considered unnecessary and delay dangerous. A company that did not obey faced fines and other punishment. There was a clear link between cause and effect. Hawkins addressed why so many believe the system needs to be changed, and cited not stories of untreated waste discharges, but of people feeling loss of control over their land due to increased needs for environmental protection. He also wrote of individuals forced into bankruptcy due to environmental liabilities, of companies required to spend millions for limited environmental benefits, and of communities waiting for decades for the clean up of hazardous waste sites while lawyers battle in court.

Hawkins identified gaps in basic protection and explained that 80 percent of the degradation of the U.S. water today is accounted for by non-regulated, non-point source pollution or is unregulated. He claimed that EPA is aware of the fact that its agenda does not coincide with the comparative risks, and that this was documented in 1987 by a comparative risk evaluation and more recently by the National Academy of Public Administration (NAPA), in a report called *Setting Priorities, Getting Results: A New Direction for EPA*, funded by EPA, and published in April 1995. He explained that the rules have become so specific that decisions made concerning one rule often overlap and make no sense when considered in the context of the others.

He then described a move toward "environmental protection by enforcement of minor infractions," and how originally Congress understood that compliance would only be guaranteed by rigorous prosecution of non-compliance. Hawkins argues that an enforcement system for environmental laws should be based on deterrence as well as retribution, that society wants the number of violations to decrease, and that a society would be crazy to judge the success of an enforcement enterprise on its ability to maintain a certain level of violations. Yet, the numbers of inspections, fines, and penalties counted each year at EPA, and a drop in the number is often associated with a lack of effort by the region, rather than a natural progression in a successful enforcement program. As a result, many EPA agencies are forced to maintain numbers, and since progress is being made to diminish the gross offenses and such offenses are becoming harder and harder to find, EPA must then make up the difference by citing regulated organizations for less significant violations.

Robert Susman, former Deputy Administrator of EPA, said that creation of a new *integrated environmental statute* could serve to allow EPA, state agencies, the regulatory community, and public interest organizations to make numerous changes to current environmental protection practices.[63] The statute would not replace other federal environmental statutes, but would change how the regulation would be applied and carried out. He underscored the need to promote flexibility in the responses of various regulated communities. The Aspen Institute in Washington produced a report resulting from a 3 year program of discussion between environmentalist union officials and industry representatives.[64] The report claims that an alternative regulatory track in which businesses can negotiate tougher than regulation performance standards with community representatives in exchange for regulatory flexibility, could enhance environmental protection and reduce costs. CIBA-Geigy, Monsanto, 3M, Union Carbide, and EPA helped fund the program.

Pennsylvania Governor, Thomas Ridge, is ready to explore alternative regulatory tracks and is calling for vision and action. He says it is time to end the confrontational and legalistic mystery of environmental protection.[65] He calls for a new approach committed to seeking meaningful input from stakeholders and encourages regulatory negotiation and opening of government to new ideas. He identifies information as an essential element, and indicates his intention to move away from an attitude of "government knows best," and toward shared responsibility for a clean environment. He encourages environmental compliance audits and voluntary, self-policing environmental management systems, declares that it is time to move beyond command-and-control, and maintains that global environmental performance is only possible through partnership.

EPA's Response to the Call for Change

In an announcement of EPA's Common Sense Initiative, EPA Administrator Carol M. Browner is quoted as saying:

> We want to make good on what business and environmentalists have been telling us for two decades, that we must look at whole facilities, whole industries and their overall impact on the environment. We must do a better job of cleaning up the environment and do it cheaper.[66]

Claiming that today's environmental problems require a new approach, the current approach was criticized for supporting two obstacles to comprehensive environmental protection. The first was that innovation and common sense are stifled by the complicated and rigid system; for example, a typical small business may be subject to as many as ten major environmental statutes that require dozens of reports without getting the best results. The second obstacle is that complexity and rigidity breed conflict, and adversarial relationships often resulting in gridlock. EPA affirmed its commitment to change and explained its definition of what it means by reinventing itself.[67] It claimed that it would reshape its environmental protections to make them simpler and more sensible to regulatory entities, include stakeholders in developing new, more effective, less costly approaches, and emphasize environmental results, not the fulfillment of regulatory mandates as its primary goal. Again, it stated that flexibility, good stewardship, and strong partnerships between the public and private sectors inspired better solutions to environmental problems.

Apparently in response to some of the recommendations in the *Reinventing Environmental Regulations* report that accompanies the *National Performance Review* (NPRRER), EPA, for the first time, asked states to participate in the drafting of the enforcement agreements that EPA–Washington signs with its regional offices.[68] Better partnership is the goal of this effort. Getting states involved is likely to shift focus from the fulfilling of national goals to addressing local and regional concerns. Some states are skeptical that EPA can be flexible enough to allow the states to influence its enforcement programs. However, since the states now do the vast majority of the environmental enforcement, it may be hard for EPA to hold the reigns too tightly.

Fred Hansen, Deputy Administrator of EPA, asked, "How shall we improve the system used to protect human health and the environment, so that it generates more benefits … while imposing less cost?"[69] He acknowledged that the current system may not be the best suited to current environmental challenges, and that the EPA must evolve. Furthermore, he asserted that improvements are necessary and called for by voices across the political spectrum. According to Hansen, EPA is in the midst of fundamental reassessment and change, but that the sweeping changes that the American public and the President are looking for cannot be unilateral. Simultaneous and corresponding changes must occur in government and business, and environmental safeguards should not be diminished during the process of change.

Hansen referenced the NPRRER, March 16, 1995, as providing a useful framework for reassessment and change. NPRRER asserted that "EPA is hobbled by overly prescriptive statutes," and recommended that EPA present Congress with a proposal for an integrated environmental statute that would allow the agency to set priorities and integrate programs across environmental media. NPRRER recommends that EPA grant more responsibility to environmental stakeholders, and while EPA would retain the authority to set and enforce national standards and assure accountability, states would have more responsibility for managing environmental programs and regulated businesses.

He discussed development of a new management system for EPA that would allow it to set its priorities based on risk and other relevant factors, and change those priorities in response to new demands. He mentioned that members of the Senate Appropriations Committee have been frustrated and dissatisfied because EPA is taking so much time to reinvent itself, and because EPA seems reluctant to produce a timetable that lays out milestones. He indicated that Administrator Browner and he shared their frustration but at the same time pointed out that it is a process not a project, and that many of the changes will be subtle. Reinvention is an evolutionary process of cultural change that by its nature is time intensive. It takes more time to build partnerships and develop the groundwork for broad consensus than it does to write regulations.

Privatizing Environmental Protection

A new wave in privatization is focusing on the development of tools to be used by regulated companies to achieve regulatory compliance.[70] In this development, command-and-control strategies are supplanted by marketplace forces. Goals include reduced compliance costs, increased business efficiency, and good public relations. In view of the potential benefits both to regulators and to the regulated community, it is likely that voluntary environmental management programs will become an integral component of our overall environmental protection system.

The chemical industry's Responsible Care Program has encouraged chemical firms to form partnerships with communities to invite third-party audits to show what the firms are doing and how they are controlling pollution, as well as to illustrate how more can be accomplished.[71] To reduce the fear that results of third party audits will be used against environmentally responsible organizations, the state of South Carolina is considering legislation that would prevent the use of such findings to incriminate firms and individuals for violations voluntarily discovered and corrected.

The most prominent among a number of voluntary private-sector environmental initiatives is the new International Organization for Standardization's ISO 14001 Environmental Management System Standard.[72] ISO 14001 was approved as a final standard in September 1996 and was adopted immediately thereafter by the 15 state members of the European Union (EU). The EU voted unanimously to accept it as the sole European standard for environmental management systems.[73] Japan's Ministry of International Trade and Industry (MITI) asked its nation's companies to prepare new environmental management plans by the end of 1996 that will conform to the ISO 14001.[74] Prompted by a concern that they not be shut out of the global market, and in response to MITI's request, Toyota, Sony Chemical, Ricoh, Canon, Fujitsu, and Nippon Petroleum became the first Japanese companies to be certified to the ISO 14001 standard.[75] Many other countries are moving rapidly towards adoption of the international standard and it is anticipated that ISO 14001 will become the worldwide standard for environmental operations.[76] This likelihood holds the sharp interest of U.S. corporations who have significant involvement in international trade.

One example is Lucent Technologies (formerly AT&T Microelectronics) which through its participation in EPA's Project XL will test the ISO 14001 certification pilot program as an alternate strategy for ensuring environmental protection. Lucent will certify all of its 13 worldwide manufacturing locations to the ISO 14001 Environmental Management System Standard and use several of its facilities as test sites for regulatory relief programs. Lucent has indicated that it is likely to require its suppliers to conform to at least portions of the ISO 14001.[77] Companies like IBM are moving towards "registration-ready" status (i.e., where all systems are in place, but for which certification has not yet been sought),[78] and the ISO standard is very likely to be adopted by most major U.S. industries involved in international trade.[79] Yet, this shift requires industry to take on more responsibility for protecting the environment, and essential to that step is the issue of trust, not only for government to industry but for industry to government as well.[80] Industrial managers need to determine whether they can work collaboratively with government regulators and whether they can trust their competition to live up to comparable standards.[81]

In the words of James Sief, Secretary of Pennsylvania's Department of Environmental Protection, "In today's global economy, initiatives from European governments and the private-sector to adopt these standards [ISO 14000] are creating market pressures on both large companies and small suppliers to meet ISO 14000 or be locked out of key markets."[82] Sief said that the 14000 also represents the next generation of environmental protection tools, those needed to achieve our goals. He identified it as an opportunity and lauded it as a new way of using performance based objectives, positive incentives, external validation, and flexibility to continuously improve and seek new opportunities. He said, "It's only by using these next generation tools that we can achieve the zero discharge goal we recently adopted as the ultimate objective..." and that the ISO 14000 is potentially many times more effective than command-and-control methods for achieving significant environmental improvements.

According to Sief, ISO will essentially privatize environmental regulation, since it ensures that companies have internalized regulatory concepts and that they set up effective structures to improve environmental performance at lower and lower environmental costs. In addition, public reporting and accountability toward meeting environmental goals are built into the process, much like Underwriters Laboratories for setting standards for electrical products and ASTM for environmental review and materials standards, both which are private groups. He identified the government role as defining the minimum environmental results to be achieved, and that government regulations need to be changed to become more performance based and less prescriptive.

Pennsylvania is looking at how inspection and permitting policies should change for organizations certified to ISO, how laws and regulations should be changed to accommodate the ISO system, how DEP can work with the public to help understand what the new approach to environmental protection means, and how smaller companies can be included in the program.

He quotes Carol A. Ritter, Vice President, Environmental and General Services for AMP Inc., a major manufacturer of electric components as saying:

> The overwhelming benefits of a standard of this type is that it will allow a company to be proactive and get ahead of the regulatory curve; to eliminate the materials, processes and wastes that subject a company to regulation; and to subject competition, particularly off-shore competition, to a similar set of environmental principles that U.S. companies have been dealing with for many years. In the long term, this means bottom line dollar savings to most companies, but the time to get started is now!

Sief proclaimed his pleasure at having companies like Ritter's and Lucent Technologies within his state to work on moving in this direction. Common characteristics for this new set of tools would include that they:

- ❑ are performance based, and do not dictate specific solutions
- ❑ use positive incentives
- ❑ encourage innovation
- ❑ look for new opportunities
- ❑ rely heavily on education and training
- ❑ redirect resources to where they will yield the most benefit
- ❑ require strong management commitment
- ❑ encourage public reporting and accountability
- ❑ are voluntary

Examples of these tools include the following:

Environmental Compliance Audits — Companies conducting compliance audits or achieving ISO 14001 certification will be protected from fines or penalties for violations they uncover as long as they report them and promptly correct them (this would not apply to more serious violations or where there have been patterns of non-compliance).

Facility-wide Permits — State and company would look at what steps can be taken to reduce or eliminate pollution throughout the plant; it focuses on putting money and resources where they will be most effective.

Customer Needs Surveys — State would look at specific companies or industries and determine where it makes the most sense to spend time, including the concept of facility-wide permitting.

Pennsylvania's Department of Environmental Protection has adopted the theme, "Taking the next step!" to highlight this shift to the new generation of tools.

Steven A. Herman, Assistant Administrator, EPA, identified the emergence of ISO 14001, Voluntary Industry Standard for Environmental Management Systems, as raising important environmental enforcement and compliance issues on federal and state levels.[83] He proposed establishing a single quorum to discuss and develop recommendations concerning these issues as they specifically relate to 14001. He stated that through EPA's long term standards network is, headed up by the Office of Prevention, Pesticides and Toxic Substances, EPA has encouraged the development and use of voluntary industry standards including ISO 14001 and other 14000 standards. He explained that EPA is exploring the benefit of environmental management systems and several of its own initiatives, citing the environmental leadership program (ELP) and Project XL as examples. He stated that several applicants of these existing programs have indicated that they plan to become ISO 14001 registered and have sought regulatory benefits in exchange for ISO registration, and that several states have expressed their interest in the ISO registration as a means complementing their existing compliance programs and enforcement efforts as well as to leverage their scarce environmental resources.

EPA's Office of Enforcement and Compliance Assistance established an ISO 14001 EMS Task Group for the purposes of:

- ❑ developing recommendations regarding the relationship between the EPA Audit/Self-Policing policies systematic discovery criteria for compliance management systems (CMS) and ISO 14001
- ❑ developing recommendations regarding other enforcement and compliance issues related to EMS/ISO 14001
- ❑ providing a forum for information exchange and coordination among state and federal environmental enforcement and compliance officials with respect to EMS/ISO programs and projects

EPA's Voluntary Environmental Programs

To encourage companies to conduct voluntary, comprehensive environmental compliance activities, the U.S. Environmental Protection Agency has instituted a variety of *partnership* policies and programs under which EPA promises to work "cooperatively with the private sector to provide stakeholders with effective tools to address environmental issues." [84] These include:[85]

33/50 — 1991 — The first partnership program was successful at reducing release of 33 percent of 17 toxic chemicals by 1992, and 50 percent by 1995.

Design for the Environment — 1991 — To help businesses incorporate environmental considerations into the design and redesign of products, processes, and technical and management systems.

Green Lights — 1991 — To prevent pollution by encouraging U.S. institutions to use energy-efficient lighting technologies.

Environmental Accounting Program — 1992 — To encourage and motivate business to understand the full spectrum of their environmental costs, and integrate these costs into decision making.

Agstar — 1993 — To promote cost-effective methods for reducing methane emissions through manure management.

Common Sense Initiative — 1993/94 — Sets up teams of representatives from governments, environmental groups, labor, and industry to look for opportunities to change complicated and inconsistent environmental regulations into comprehensive strategies for environmental protection, with an emphasis on pollution prevention, instead of end-of-pipe solutions, at less cost to taxpayers and industry.

Environmental Leadership Program — 1994 — To recognize and provide incentives to facilities willing to develop and demonstrate innovative approaches to establishing accountability for compliance with existing laws.

Pesticide Environmental Stewardship Program — 1994 — To develop specific use/risk reduction strategies that include reliance on approaches to pest control that are thought to be safer than traditional chemical methods.

Green Chemistry Program — 1995 — To recognize and promote fundamental breakthroughs in chemistry that accomplish pollution prevention in a cost effective manner.

Project XL Program — 1995 — EPA's "flagship" program. To give regulated sources the flexibility to develop alternative strategies that will replace or modify specific regulatory requirements on the condition that they produce greater environmental benefits.

President Clinton created the Project XL program on March 16, 1995 to provide the flexibility to develop common sense, cost-effective strategies to replace regulatory requirements when such alternatives are likely to produce greater environmental benefits.[86] The program is based on the premise that participants will know better than the federal government how to reduce their pollution and it promises to reduce the regulatory burden and promote economic growth while achieving better environmental and public health protection. The President promised:

> We will provide the flexibility to test alternative strategies to achieve environmental goals ... Responsible companies will be given the flexibility to develop alternative strategies that will replace current regulatory requirements, while producing even greater environmental benefits.[87]

In March of 1996, the EPA offered the challenge that if a company can exceed regulatory standards for environmental performance, EPA will provide flexibility and cut red tape so that it can find the cheapest way to do so.[88]

EPA acknowledged that flexibility and collaboration can produce increased environmental benefits at reduced costs.[89] In a solicitation for Project XL project proposals, EPA explained that it will require the participation of state agencies as full partners with EPA, and that EPA is taking a decentralized or franchising approach to the implementation of the program — yet it makes clear that this authority is being delegated by EPA. According to the solicitation, important elements of the project include an estimate of the likely outcome and an explicit statement concerning what data and analyses are needed to determine success. It clearly states that these estimates are likely to be uncertain due to scientific and/or engineering questions as well as to interpretation of the future applicable regulatory requirements. This is quite different than demanding that a company guarantee certain environmental results prior to EPA approving the project. It explains that the purpose of XL is to provide alternatives to existing regulations in exchange for superior environmental performance.

In its Statement of Regulatory Priorities, EPA affirms its commitment to change, and explains its definition of what it means by reinventing itself.[90] It claims that it intends to reshape its environmental protections to make them simpler and more sensible to regulatory entities, to include stakeholders in developing new, more effective, less costly approaches, and emphasize environmental results, not the fulfillment of regulatory mandates, as its primary goal. It states that flexibility, good stewardship, and strong partnerships between the public and private sectors inspire better solutions to environmental problems. The statement of priorities goes on to claim that EPA is building a new system that will use innovative, non-prescriptive, consensus-based techniques to achieve environmental goals beyond those set by existing laws. EPA offers the challenge that if a company can exceed regulatory standards for environmental performance, EPA will provide flexibility and cut red tape so that it can find the cheapest way to do that. Gordon Moore, Chairman of the Board, Intel Corporation, states:

> What I see in Project XL is a real paradigm shift...just think of the environmental gains we could make if we tap into the creativity that put 5.5 million transistors on a chip the size of your thumbnail![91]

EPA claimed that it will seek full partnership with state environmental agencies in the Project XL program and has already approved a proposal to recognize the State of Minnesota as a partner and empower it to manage the XL program.[92]

In response to the question, "How is XL different from the Amoco Yorktown Project?," EPA said it is different because the XL program came down from the President, it is a top priority of the Administrator, and it will be run by the Regions and the states.[93] In a description of the Lucent Technologies project, on its World Wide Web Homepage, EPA explained that Lucent intends to certify its environmental management system to 14001 as its Project XL proposal. Lucent proposed using the EMS as a framework for developing simplified permitting, record keeping, and reporting requirements in a multi-regional attempt to incorporate environmental management practices into its business management systems. This effort incorporates EPA Regions 3, 4, and 6 and according to Lucent there has been some difficulty in getting collaboration among the three.

EPA Office of Enforcement and Compliance Assistance has proposed using portions of the ISO 14001 Standards as the basis of the environmental management standards for its Environmental Leadership Program and has asked the American National Standards Institute (ANSI is the U.S. representative body to the ISO for the 14000 standard) for permission to use portions of the ISO 14001 verbatim in its own document.[94]

Pennsylvania, California, Wisconsin, Minnesota, New Jersey, Massachusetts, Illinois, North Carolina, and Texas formed a group to coordinate efforts to develop pilot programs to test ISO 14000 with respect to state regulatory programs.[95] Other government policies and programs, like EPA's Audit Policy and Environmental Leadership Program, promote the use of self-policing activities by promising deferred or diminished penalties for environmental violations.[96] State-level initiatives, such as those under development in Connecticut[97] and Pennsylvania,[98] may also include environmental audit privileges and amnesty programs. In most cases, existence of an environmental management system is a prerequisite for consideration under these opportunities. EPA-Region I's *Environmental Leadership Program* offers amnesty for violations, less frequent inspections, and regulatory relief for companies that exceed regulatory requirements through pollution prevention. *EPA's Incentives for Self-Policing: Discovery, Disclosure, Correction and Prevention of Violations* (Federal Register, December 22, 1995) offers protection from gravity-based and criminal penalties for environmental violations discovered during self-monitoring type activities conducted under a voluntary environmental management system.

EPA's Voluntary Program Problems

In spite of the substantial commitment to encourage voluntary environmental performance, EPA is drawing increased criticism from leading U.S. industries and states who claim that current environmental regulations and the structure or regulatory programs and agencies, significantly obstruct efforts to improve environmental performance. The most oft-cited example of such obstruction is the Yorktown Refinery case.

Reporting in the *Environmental Law Reporter*, William F. Pedersen, Jr., explains that in 1993, under the then current regulatory framework, the Amoco Yorktown Refinery, in Yorktown, Pennsylvania, was required to reduce about 7,300 tons of airborne hydrocarbon emissions per year at a cost of $2,400 per ton.[99] AMOCO found that by using control strategies different than those required by the regulations, it could eliminate 7,500 tons per year of the same hydrocarbons and more dangerous hazardous waste for an average cost of only $500 per ton, about one-fifth of the cost of the action required by law. According to Pedersen, EPA did not and still does not have the statutory authority to approve the Yorktown alternative or any other multimedia pollution reduction strategies like it. He says that this demonstrates that because major sources have been regulated intensely for over a generation, under the law of diminishing returns, the ability of such a blunt instrument, as is embodied in current regulation, to achieve further reductions is decreasing steadily. That is an argument for pollution prevention as a more likely method of reducing pollution, but he stipulates that companies must have the freedom to produce these reductions where they are available, not where the government says they should be. Another point he makes is that the regulations are without defensible goals. This is because regulations are not designed to correspond to an environmental goal but rather to require specified control technology. There is little connection with the cost as a criterion for deciding upon environmental controls.

In *The Death of Common Sense: How Law is Suffocating America*, Philip K. Howard, explains how, using the Amoco Yorktown Refinery as an example, EPA's regulation was so precisely drawn that it missed the major source of pollution, which in this case was the atmospheric emissions resulting from gasoline fuel being pumped into the barges at the loading dock.[100] He argues that regulators cannot see the forest for the trees, and argues for goal-oriented regulations under which a polluter could devise its own strategy for meeting the goal.

The Yorktown project is a particularly interesting case study because it was conducted by Amoco in partnership with EPA for the purpose of demonstrating the first comprehensive assessment of air emissions from a single industrial facility. EPA was criticized for its role in this effort, not only because it took enforcement action against Amoco on a different matter while the project was underway, but even more so because it was unable to take any constructive action when the study revealed large, unregulated emission sources at the loading operation that were capable of being controlled more effectively and efficiently than were the regulated emissions.

A Floundering Flagship

In setting forth its regulatory reform strategy, the Clinton Administration proposed to reinvent environmental protection for the 21st century.[101] It declared that we now know that pollution represents economic inefficiency and that profits can be increased by preventing pollution. It acknowledged the limitations of the end-of-the-pipe approach and explained how its inflexible nature results in costly actions that defy common sense and require greater costs than are necessary for smaller returns on investment, all the while discouraging technological innovation. It called for new and innovative ways to achieve greater levels of environmental protection at a lower cost. As examples, it proposed the use of performance standards rather than in combination with operational standards. This would allow the regulated community to figure out how to best meet the performance standards. It called for accountability and responsibility as natural accompaniments to increased flexibility to provide the public with confidence that their environmental goals are being met. It talked about how the adversarial approach tends to preclude innovation, and how collaborative decision-making can create bridges to reach new solutions. EPA's Project XL was identified as the regulatory reform *flagship,* the spearhead of the Administration's alternative strategies to achieve environmental goals.

Notwithstanding its statements of vision and commitment to the Project XL initiative, EPA's efforts have been found by many to be inadequate. Kenneth Chilton, Director of the Center for the Study of American Business at Washington University in St. Louis, argues for economic incentives to replace bureaucratic coercion as the dominant force behind environmental programs.[102] He points out how the current regulatory system tends to deny companies the opportunity to innovate, and that such opportunity would have resulted in lower overall emissions at the Yorktown refinery. He also calls for statutory changes to provide the flexibility that is promised in Project XL and the Common Sense Initiative programs.

On August 27, 1996, the Minnesota Pollution Control Agency's, Acting Commissioner, Peder Larson, informed EPA Administrator, Carol Browner, that the state may withdraw from the Project XL pilot program unless significant differences were resolved.[103-104] Larson explained that in spite of the Administration's claims that the XL program was the common sense way to reduce regulation and increase environmental protection at less cost, EPA's insistence on prescriptive permit conditions would have rendered the experimental nature of the project moot. On September 9, 1996, the Minnesota Mining & Manufacturing Company (3M), shelved its Project XL proposal, accusing EPA of clinging to command-and-control procedures.[105] Commissioner Larson repeated that EPA had been untrue to its own slogan about its openness to innovation, and charged that it was inflexible and failed to entrust 3M, a company with a proven record of "exemplary environmental performance," to assume responsibility and accountability for demonstrating that the Project XL flexibility will produce superior environmental performance. He claimed that EPA required the permit to contain restrictive and burdensome conditions under which failure to achieve a single superior environmental performance test would be grounds for amendment or revocation of the permit prior to the end of its 5 year term. Minnesota had been the only state approved for a pilot XL project aimed at granting state entities flexibility in achieving environmental goals. Larsen claimed that EPA would allow only XL projects containing up-front guarantees for superior performance to proceed. 3M proposed a single permit for the management of air, water, and hazardous waste discharges in order to simplify reporting and paperwork and save money, but the negotiations halted when, in contrast to the language of EPA's solicitation which requires only that a "project include an estimate of the likely outcome," EPA demanded that 3M guarantee environmental improvements.[106] 3M explained that it could not afford to delay the plant upgrades pending resolution of the dispute with EPA and that a traditional approach, conventional permitting process, would have been quicker.[107]

While Project XL is supposed to symbolize EPA's shift away from command-and-control dictates and toward common sense approaches and pollution control strategies developed in the field, the old ways appear to be dying hard.[108] The MPCA is the only state-level participant in the first round of the program and it suspended its Project XL efforts to develop a multimedia permit with 3M. 3M is doubtful that this will be worked out.

Industry representatives have expressed their frustration at EPA's inflexibility in the 3M project.[109] Eleven months of negotiations over how to guarantee the project will improve the environment resulted in gridlock. 3M claimed that EPA would not recognize the fact that their plants already had pollution controls in place that exceeded the current standards. Ryan Delcambre, Director of Environmental and Health Regulatory Affairs at Dow Chemical, said that the ten months it took to get their project approved throws doubt as to whether it was more or less cumbersome than the conventional permitting process. Deputy Assistant Administrator, Lisa Lund, acknowledged that the implementation of the program needs to be streamlined and that the agency did not speak with one voice on Project XL. Patricia Kenworthy, Director of Regulatory Affairs for Monsanto, said that while the difficulties at 3M are disheartening they do demonstrate the importance of the pilot program.

Citing the failure of Project XL as an example, the Republican staff of the House Transportation and Infrastructure Committee charged that EPA's attempt to reinvent itself has neither saved money nor resulted in a single change in EPA regulations.[110] They charged that the 3M/Minnesota Project XL pilot project was scuttled by EPA when it could not be fit into a command-and-control box, and claimed that while EPA was looking at alternative programs they were ignoring the identifiable flaws in the current structure.

At an October 31, 1996 meeting of bipartisan officials from environmental organizations in 13 states, Carol Browner was told that Project XL was "going nowhere."[111] Massachusetts environmental commissioner, David Struhs, charged that a disconnection existed between senior agency officials program staff. Ross Harding, Deputy Director of the Michigan Department of Natural Resources, described Project XL as a moving target, and extremely poorly managed at every level. He said, "It's dead in Michigan. There is so much suspicion on the part of the regulated community that it's not worth spending much time on it anymore." Browner agreed to create a new task force to identify alternative ways to accelerate regulatory innovation. The task force will be coordinated by Peter Larson of Minnesota, Randall Mathis of Arkansas' Department of Pollution Control and Ecology, and EPA's Deputy Administrator Fred Hansen.

EPA Administrator Browner claims that some mid-course corrections are being made[112] but owners of industrial plants have complained that EPA is too enforcement oriented for a voluntary program to succeed.[113] As of December 9, 1996, only two companies had reached implementation stage in spite of the fact that in April 1995, President Clinton set a target of approving 50 projects. There are 24 proposals still in the pipeline but 15 of the original proposals have dropped out for a variety of reasons. Some identify conflicts with the EPA as a major issues; others say the lack of structure and precise definition makes agreement difficult.

State environmental officials, acting under the auspices of the Environmental Council of the States (ECOS), passed a resolution charging EPA with the mishandling of Project XL.[114] Complaints were about the process used to select projects, the substance of the XL permits, and the inability of EPA staff to give final approval for the projects without intervention of top agency officials.[115] The National Governor's Association supported ECOS with a September 16, 1996 letter to EPA's Project XL staff.[116] States, acting through the Environmental Council of States, have charged that EPA is not taking into consideration the differences among state-specific approaches to environmental protection, and that EPA's criticisms [of state-sponsored environmental audit privilege policies] indicate that EPA does not fully understand the state laws.[117]

In response to a concern that EPA did not have the legislative authority to implement Project XL as intended and that it did not have the ability to provide the flexibility that it promised, an Agency representative stated that while it was true that EPA lacks the Congressional authority it needs to deliver on this promise, it does have some mechanisms in place.[118] He envisioned these steps as a ladder, the analogy being that with each step of the ladder you are higher and you can see farther, but there is more of a likelihood that if you fall you will get hurt. At the bottom of the ladder is what is considered creative interpretation of the existing regulations. He referred to the Intel Corporation as an example of this in which creative interpretations of the Clean Air Act, RCRA, and the Clean Water Act were applied. The second rung up on the ladder was described as creative interpretation of the statute. Gaps may exist between the law and the regulation and EPA may have interpreted the law more stringently or more extensively than needed. EPA can draft a rule specific to a company's situation. The Merck Company and Weyerhaeuser were cited as examples of that level of mechanism. At the highest rung of the ladder is enforcement discretion, based on the argument that EPA has limited resources so it has to make decisions about which laws it will enforce and which it will not, and that they can use this to make a decision not to enforce a particular law at a site. This approach is avoided, however, because individuals can bring *citizen suits* against companies and against EPA.

In response to the concerns that there may be an inherent conflict in EPA being both a collaborative partnership-type of organization and a regulating entity, and that EPA couldn't legitimately enter into collaboration with other states and organizations and claim to give the others equal status in negotiation when EPA is in fact the one delegating the authority and retains the power to pull it back, an EPA representative explained that EPA will not use the XL program as a sting operation; it is not a trick to get inside and see what is going on.[119] Regarding EPA's need to maintain 'tight-fisted' control, he said they were moving away from that and again used the example of the Intel Corporation where there was some multi-jurisdictional issues with the state, the locality had various interests, and EPA was just one of the players in that situation. He said one of the real questions that they are having problems with is what is the appropriate role of all the stakeholders. EPA would like to bring decision making to the community. He added that one other conundrum is trying to determine who the appropriate stakeholders are in any situation, and what process to follow to make sure that they have their say.

8

The Potential of Voluntary Environmental Management

How Do You Spell Regulatory Relief?

General agreement exists that administrative paperwork-type of regulatory requirements are likely candidates for replacement by alternate systems that achieve the same ends. Significant trade-offs can be expected when government-dictated forms and procedures are replaced with those that are organization-specific.

> We're talking about all the administrative, bureaucratic, safeguards that have been established that give regulators some assurance that companies are doing the right things. We're looking at those things. Those are the things that are the impediments for companies — to change their processes; to do their work; and all that kind of thing (SG).

The next level of regulatory relief involves easing some of the rigors of the permitting process.

> Companies are not, for the most part, complaining about the actual levels of environmental protection. It's the things that go with those that are the bothersome things. Those are the things that we have to get rid of or moderate to a large extent. It's the inspections, it's the reports, it's the number of permits, it's the frequency of permits, it's the detail of permits (SG).

Some possible alternatives to the current system include: issuance of continuous permits that remain in effect as long as specified conditions are met, bubble permits which involve "permitting an entire plant with performance indicators for the plant, [rather than the current process of] … detailing a smokestack here, a smokestack there, this process, that process" (ISO), relying on EMS reports and audits to determine levels of compliance as alternative to inspections, and relying on an agency-approved company to control its facility's emissions through its own internal permit system.

While EPA officials made it clear that there is no official Agency policy on ISO 14000 at this time, there was a willingness to discuss potential components that might be included in such a policy, were it to be developed. Included in such speculations were: less burdensome strategies for environmental monitoring and reporting, expediency in the permitting process, fewer or less vexatious inspections, diminished or deferred penalties for violations, increased flexibility, and generally preferential status and treatment. The general sense was that there was optimism that there would eventually be a connection between certification to ISO 14001 and satisfaction of some EPA requirements:

> Officially, we have really nothing to say; we're looking at all the options. Unofficially, I think there is great potential in terms of reporting and monitoring since that can be much more efficiently done through a multi-media approach. I think government procurement is a very big area (EPA).

> In terms of regulatory benefits, I really hesitate to say. What I am hearing from our enforcement offices and from our program offices, like the Office of Water, people that I work with, is speeding up of permitting and the ability of the system to help a company make use of existing privileges is about where the vision stops at this point. But they fully anticipate that given some experience in some pilot projects, they'll be able to identify other, more aggressive areas (EPA).

The term "given some experience" was repeated in several forms by individuals in different sectors and "some experience" may be a central and requisite element in the process of change at EPA. An NGO representative agreed, "regulatory relief will lag ISO's implementation, it will not precede it" (NGO). And, a corporate environmental director felt, "it's a little early to tell just how far it's going to go" (IEM). At the state level, agency officials voiced similar concerns, "what we're doing in NY is to say, we don't want to jump in feet first, because, we know it's there but we don't know how deep the lake is" (SG). Even in Pennsylvania, which unquestionably is one of the most progressive states in this regard, officials are looking first to see some evidence that these new initiatives will enhance environmental performance. An official from the Pennsylvania Department of Environmental Protection identified: reduced reporting requirements, diminished or deferred penalties for violations, and expedited permitting all as areas for potential regulatory benefits, but added that such benefits should be bestowed, "only based on their [i.e., industry's] actions" (SG).

Pennsylvania has adopted a rather unique perspective in that, rather than focusing on how to transfer responsibility for ensuring environmental regulatory compliance from government to industry, the approach is to encourage industry to extricate itself from the regulatory web altogether. Pennsylvania's carefully worded description of this approach states that, "The benefits are what a company chooses to do to work its way out of being regulated" (SG).

Which Comes First?

The complexity of agency decision-making regarding how to respond to ISO 14000 is exacerbated by industry's malleable position on the same issue. Conversely, industry is waiting for an agency position on the standard in order to solidify its approach:

> We ... know from dealing with the regulated community people that they don't have all the answers either. As an example in the ISO 14000 arena, one story that I like to tell is that when Cascio was ... at IBM, ... and he's ... Mr. ISO and he's chair of the TC207 and everything else, and yet when he worked for IBM all those years IBM had still not decided whether they're going to participate. Because they've got an environmental management system in place. So they're going slow, they're going deliberate, they're looking, 'What does this buy us if we go in? Do we need it for our competitive places in the global market?' and they haven't made all the decisions yet (SG).

Regarding the same example, Mr. Cascio had almost exactly the same comments:

> Before I left IBM my vice president said, "What the hell do we want to do this for?" I said there is going to be all kinds of regulatory flexibility. He says, "Well, where's the regulatory flexibility?" I said, "It's not here yet. The regulators want to know that this is actually working and that we're taking it seriously so then they can give us regulatory flexibility." He says, "I'm not going to spend $1 million a plant on a supposition that I'm going to get some regulatory flexibility" (ISO).

The learning curve is quite steep from the time an organization begins looking at the ISO 14000 until the time that a decision is made that it has merit, but from that point until steps are taken to begin implementing it, it flattens out very quickly:

> It is a chicken and egg syndrome here. Industry is saying they want some evidence that this is important. The environmentalists and the government are saying, we can't give you benefits until we know that this is working and its really making you behave in a more consistent and a more responsible way.... And the two sides are kind of facing each other off and saying, 'well you make a move' (ISO).

It appears likely that industry will have to make the first move in order to provide some examples of demonstrated success. Government should be involved closely in such demonstrations. Such collaboration could provide some degree of confidence for outside observers that environmental quality standards are being maintained.

A Call for Leadership

Widespread adoption of the ISO 14001 EMS in the U.S. will be restrained if industry cannot see that there is some benefit from government. Industry and state governments have become frustrated with the anemic effort of EPA to support voluntary environmental performance. There is a call for proactive governmental leadership:

> Government ... which is presumably the leadership level ... ought to be the ones to show some leadership here. They ought to be the ones that take the chance and show leadership and say, 'Okay, this is what we're going to give you guys.' Oh, they don't have to give you anything. They could just say, 'This is what we're offering. We're going to offer you this kind of flexibility and we expect you to accomplish this. If you don't accomplish this, within a certain time, and all that sort of thing, then we're going to take the flexibility away.' They can do that. They can do it provisionally. They don't have to do it absolutely. But it seems to me that with a little bit of imagination, and a little bit of leadership and a little bit of guts, the government could take a lead on this (ISO).

EPA has responded to this call by setting up various task groups and advisory committees to try and "iron out" the problems that the agency is having upholding its end of the partnership. The results of such efforts are lessened by the agency's concurrent attempt to satisfy a call from its environmental advocacy constituency for more active enforcement.

Certification to ISO 14000 may increase access to other government programs like EPA's Environmental Leader Program or EPA Region 1's Star Tracks. Such considerations give rise to the issue of to what extent the agency waives other eligibility criteria in lieu of ISO certification. Another issue is whether ISO certification should become a prerequisite for eligibility for other programs. Under most EPA sponsored volunteer programs, participating companies must have an environmental management system in place:

> I think it is one of the strengths of the ISO to have one system that you can get to know well enough so that you don't have to reinvent the wheel ... I would hesitate to say that would be the only way that you could get on the Star Track, but there are distinct advantages to having a standard way (EPA).

While agencies are hesitant to sanction any one EMS system, the worldwide acceptance of the ISO EMS makes it an attractive option.

Less Paperwork

An agency may require companies to prepare and submit reports because it needs the information either for existing programs or in support of a new program that it intends to launch. Occasionally, program initiatives are deferred or canceled yet the paperwork requirements are left on the books. "One of the things we've heard from a lot of companies is that DEC and other agencies make us keep all these records which don't mean anything; they don't do anything (SG)." Often the agency did not make an effort to determine whether such information already was being collected as a result of another agency requirement, or of that of another governmental body. It is argued, that left to its own devices, industry could more effectively and efficiently manage its environmental data because it could do so in a manner that corresponded with the systems in place for managing the data associated with the other aspects of its business:

> ISO would probably give them [i.e., industry] an opportunity to say, 'this is information which is important to us, it tracks the same sorts of indicators or data that ... would be necessary for you, the state, to make sure that we're in compliance. We're already tracking it, you need to come and see it and drive on by' (SG).

A significant impediment to industry taking on more responsibility for managing its environmental aspects and the data generated from those activities, is that any system it sets up to do this must be *in addition to,* rather than *in place of,* the system required by the agency or agencies governing its environmental operations. Consequently, the benefit associated with reduced paperwork is focused on how business management systems, like the ISO 14001 Environmental Management System, can satisfy the agency's need to know if a company is in compliance:

> Much of the administrative functions of regulations are ... some bureaucrat's best idea of how to get a demonstration for a regulated industry that they're in compliance ... I think that the biggest thing that could happen is that if a company is ISO certified ... we don't need to see those demonstrations anymore ... I think that has potential but it has a long way to go to get the regulator's confidence (SG).

A principal consideration for the agency under this scenario is determining what it will need to look at in order to determine if an organization is in compliance.

Moving away from the one-size-fits-all standardized agency format, it is obvious that the agency will need to develop the skills necessary to evaluate a system that is put in place by a regulated organization. The approach most commonly suggested is to periodically review the organization's assessment of its own compliance and to verify this with inspections conducted at a frequency determined as a function of the organization's performance record. Similarly, agencies will need to learn how to develop permits on a facility-wide basis, rather than by looking at individual discharge points through the singular lens of the specific regulation governing that particular media and type of discharge. An industry might be given a "cap" for a particular compound and authorization to vary releases from one point-of-discharge to another as long as the overall cap wasn't exceeded. At first glance, such custom-tailored approaches can appear onerously unworkable, but the promise is that the extra "up front" effort to work out the details will result in a reduced level of effort in the long term. Also, the savings associated with a reduced number of permits might help mitigate the increased level of effort required for site-specific considerations: "If we can negotiate all these [individual] permits, there's no reason why we can't negotiate an agreement for the entire site" (ISO).

At its core, the true agency concern may not be so much about the logistics of moving toward a facility-specific regulatory program, but rather about the discretionary quality of that effort. While the fact remains that regulators often engage in negotiation with members of the regulated community regarding reporting or permit conditions, the implicit assumption is that it is not required. Putting regulators in a position in which the underlying tenet is collaborative negotiation modifies the tactical defensibility of their position.

In addition, regulators traditionally have been reluctant to (and in many cases, prohibited from) collaborating on solutions to environmental problems for fear that if the results are unsuccessful, the organization will lay the blame at their feet. "Their biggest fear right now... is that they will be asked to play more of a consultant role" (SG). Dictates from agency commissioners requiring regulators to cooperate and collaborate represent a 180-degree reversal in policy. Without training and support, regulators feel unprepared for this change.

> The tone has been changing in the last couple of years in quite a few states. You feel their discomfort when they're on the other side of the telephone and they say at the end of the conversation, 'Now I'm supposed to ask this, is there anything we can do to help?' They really have to struggle with this (IEM).

Permitting Issues

Streamlined Permitting

Speed and flexibility are the two relief factors sought by industry with respect to permitting issues. Moreover, there appears to be considerable interest on the agency side for supporting such relief in exchange for superior environmental performance and in view of the benefits that the agency would receive from not having to police a particular organization to the extent that it must under the current arrangement. The basic concept is that a company with a strong environmental performance record and a comprehensive EMS can be trusted to keep itself in compliance: "They don't need to provide ... as much information as they normally would ... since we have so much faith in their management system, they can provide less" (EPA). A history of environmental performance exceeding minimum requirements provides the agency with added assurance that the organization's commitment is genuine. Ultimately, a company may be allowed "to self-certify for permit applications because [the agency has] reason to believe that this is a proactive company that is doing the right thing" (SG).

Flexible Permitting

There are two predominant interpretations of the meaning of permit flexibility. The one embraced by the private-sector and supported by some in government is: providing a regulated organization with opportunities to innovatively improve environmental performance or efficiency without having to spell out the details of every variation in advance in a permit application.

> They can get flexibility in permitting, 'here's the standard we want you to meet, we'll be flexible in letting you try to design a better way to meet that standard. In some cases, a way to get to the standard and go beyond the standard' (SG).

The agency provides such flexibility either by regulating discharges only and not the process, or by providing a grace period in which a company can retool or otherwise modify its systems. In the latter case, the final permit is issued after the system is in place and operating successfully. While a new or enhanced system is being developed and tested, the organization may operate with something less than a complete permit.

The other, far less popular interpretation, provides companies with opportunities for innovation, but requires all alternative technologies, processes, and materials, to be identified and permitted in advance of use. Alternatives then can be used by the company in accordance with pre-determined criteria specifying under what conditions each will be employed. There are at least three problems inherent in this approach. The first is that a company may not be aware of all the reasonable alternatives. Second, is that the company may not be in a position to anticipate changes in external factors like, availability of raw materials and variation in market demand, that might necessitate a process change. Third, a company may not want to publicize its future intention to use an innovative process or technology or a new material.

Limited Permitting

Connected both to permitting speed and flexibility, is the issue of what gets permitted. Three predominant answers exist. At one end of this range is the current system of environmental permitting that requires permit applications to identify and describe the processes that generate and treat the wastes as well as the anticipated outcome at the point of discharge. Under this system, the issues of speed and flexibility are of paramount importance to regulated industries. They are concerned about the delay that must be endured if a production process needs to be modified for legitimate, and often urgent, business reasons. Since the process is specified in the discharge permit, the permit must be modified before the company actually can implement the change.

At the other end of the range, only the actual discharges would require permits; the company would not be required to provide information on its production process. The process, in essence, would exist within a "*black box*," and the company would be free to make changes to it as it needed as long as the permitted discharge conditions were not exceeded.

> As long as they can monitor specific parameters within that site, why do they have to tell the government when they change their process? It's totally absurd that the government should know when it changes its processes. What does the government care? The government doesn't care anyway (ISO).

Government officials both at federal and state levels agree that the *black box* alternative would be unworkable for them. Policy makers interested in moving toward a new public policy approach look for means to provide the public with some assurance that it will work. This is especially true in the environmental arena where environmental advocacy groups have fought long and bitter battles for over a quarter of a century to develop and strengthen the current policy. Agencies are sensitive to the concern of the NGOs that industry may not be trustworthy, and while they are committed to collaboration and partnership, they need to be certain that new strategies are not abused.

> This goes a bit to the accountability question. While the regulated entities are in the best position of figuring out how best to do something, I just don't think the *black box* approach is good public policy. We want to know something about the management system, we want to know what type of chemicals they're using ... And it's good public policy to have that information and to make that information publicly available (EPA).

> Our position is, 'look that's public policy, that's where environmental programs derive from and there should be an openness' (SG).

Yet while the *black box* approach clearly is rejected, some movement in this direction would be supported:

> What they're [industry] really saying is, 'Be flexible with us, be practical with us.' You know if company *x* has got a manufacturing operation on its fourth floor of a building and it needs to move it to the first floor for expansion room, it doesn't need to go through a formal permit mod change to do that. They can say we did it, here it is, it's not going to result in any increased emissions, we did it because we needed to do it for business reasons (SG).

In a more complicated scenario, the industry would not just be moving a process from one location to another, but modifying it for its own business reasons. One compromise may be for the agency to require different levels of detail for the production process and for the treatment process. "Certainly we'll want much more information about the performance at the end of the process. Probably less information about the process itself" (EPA).

A middle-of-the-road alternative that appears to be garnishing support from both industry and government is a system that permits not only end-of-pipe discharges, but also requires full-disclosure of process details. The middle-of-the-road option may be a good first step.

> That, personally, is a move that I very much favor. Technology is moving a lot quicker than bureaucracy. It's been the case for a long time. The things — I will call them things for lack of a better term — that these companies are coming up with really boggles the mind. And I have heard a lot of frustrated cries from friends and colleagues saying 'we have got such a better way to deal with it, but we can't implement it because it's a process change.' ... I would be very much in favor in leaning to the middle ... but we [must] know what goes on inside the black box, it's not a black hole, it's [public] information as far as we're concerned (NGO).

This middle-ground may represent a reasonable milestone in the transformation process that is within the range of vision afforded to U.S. society from the reality platform upon which it now stands.

Enforcement Relief

EPA's *'Incentives for Self-Policing: Discovery, Disclosure, Correction and Prevention of Violations,'* (the 'Audit Policy'), published in the Federal Register on December 22, 1995, offers some protection from gravity-based and criminal penalties for environmental violations discovered during self-monitoring type activities conducted under a voluntary environmental management system. While under specified conditions, the Audit Policy provides benefits for companies without an environmental management system in place, it is clear that existence of such a system is expected. As previously discussed in detail, conformance with the specifications of the ISO 14001 EMS should satisfy the due diligence requirements for this enforcement relief benefit. In actuality, the ISO 14001 specification surpasses what is generally expected in an environmental management system. ISO 14001 provides:

> ... a comprehensive environmental management system with a pollution prevention audit and compliance audit built in ... that's a lot more than companies have to do ... And if a company really does do it and can show ... that the environment is better off, we [i.e., EPA] ought to be more forthcoming in what our enforcement relief is (EPA).

How EPA will incorporate ISO 14001 certification into its enforcement package is yet to be determined. One likely benefit "when EPA makes a final decision ... is that [ISO-certified organizations] can expect less intrusive enforcement to come their way" (NGO). If a company is doing more before they ask for any discretion, they should get a broader range of discretion in return. "It's sort of, 'you do more for me, we'll do more for you" (EPA).

Commitment to Compliance and Performance Beyond Compliance

Much of the hesitancy expressed by agency officials in response to a continuous stream of inquiries regarding what regulatory benefits are associated with ISO 14001 certification, revolves around the lack of a precise definition of the term 'commitment to compliance.' "We really need to see what is the commitment to compliance before we provide any incentives" (EPA).

One concern expressed is that ISO 14001 does not require a registrant to be in compliance with all environmental laws: "The environmental standards hold and there is nothing in ISO that requires a company to be [in] compliance with all those standards" (SG). As a condition of certification, ISO 14001 does require a company to establish 'compliance with all applicable environmental regulatory laws' as one of its goals, have an environmental management system in place capable of achieving that goal, and to commit the resources necessary for implementation.

However, a company may be out of compliance in one or more areas and still keep its certification if it is making reasonably significant progress toward the compliance goal. This gives rise to the question, "How should voluntary commitment to compliance compare to performance that might reasonably be expected under command-and-control?" Since a regulatory inspection today does not ensure that a company will be in compliance tomorrow (or was yesterday), should a voluntary effort be expected to yield more effective results? And if so, how much more? The answer is that it may not matter.

ISO 14001 is not a performance standard, it is a management standard. When an organization's EMS is evaluated by a third-party auditor, the purpose of the audit is not to determine whether the organization is in compliance, but rather, whether its EMS is appropriately designed and implemented. Therefore, the audit report could be expected to be of little use to a regulatory agency interested principally in performance. However, the information that must be collected and evaluated during a third-party review will, in fact, provide the agency with what it needs.

The National Accreditation Program (NAP) for third-party audits of ISO 14001 Environmental Management Systems,[120] requires third-party EMS auditors to insure that an organization conforms to all of ISO 14001 requirements, including compliance with environmental laws and regulations. It requires "data on compliance with relevant legislation and regulations" be collected as "relevant and necessary to determine whether the organization conforms to the standard." The auditor must verify that the organization has determined its status with regard to compliance with environmental regulatory law. NAP's disclaimer states:

> A registration audit is an audit of a management system to determine conformance to the standard and while compliance is a part of the management system, the registration audit is not an audit of full compliance with all applicable regulatory requirements.

Despite this disclaimer, these requirements, if adhered to, are likely to resolve the issue that ISO 14001 does not require an organization to be in compliance.

ISO 14001 is not an environmental performance standard. It does not specify maximum allowable concentrations of chemical parameters that can be discharged into the environment. Additionally, whether or not a company has an ISO 14001 EMS in place has no bearing on what laws and regulations with which it must comply:

> ISO 14000 is not here to replace the regulatory scheme. ISO 14000 is here to work in conjunction with the regulatory scheme because the regulatory scheme is what sets up the performance goals which the management system in the ISO 14000 allows you to work against and to meet. You can't have one without the other. A management system without performance standards is ridiculous. What are you going to manage to? It's the requirement of the regulations, principally, that set up the requirements, the goals, the objectives. The management system simply is the way for you to get there (ISO).

What the ISO 14001 EMS *will* do, according to the NAP, is require the regulated organization to determine and document its performance regarding compliance: "An organization shall … periodically evaluate compliance with relevant environmental legislation and regulations." The third-party audit provides assurance that this step is appropriately done: "The registration body shall consider whether the organization's EMS is planned and operated in a manner consistent with these requirements." As a result, what should be available for inspection by an agency is a report by a regulated organization on its own compliance status, and an evaluation of a third-party auditor regarding the veracity of that report. The agency will not have to conduct routine intrusive investigations to determine compliance status unless it has reason to suspect illicit behavior or inept performance of both organization and auditor.

Another concern expressed in response to inquiries regarding associated ISO 14001 regulatory benefits is that a company under the EMS is free to select whatever objectives and targets it would like to. This is true only to the extent that the objectives and targets are consistent with the company's environmental policy. In accordance with Section 4.2 of the ISO 14001 standard, the organization must have an environmental policy "appropriate to the nature, scale, and environmental impacts of its activities, products, or services." It must include "a commitment to continual improvement and prevention of pollution; [and] ... a commitment to comply with relevant environmental legislation and regulations ..." If an auditor determines that the company's environmental targets are inadequate or inappropriate for reaching its objectives, or that its objectives are inconsistent with its policy, the company will not be certified, or if already certified, it may lose that status.

Determining how consistent an effort is, with respect to an overall environmental policy, may be difficult and subject to various interpretations. An illustrative example can be made of a company that produces and sells two motor oil product lines, one to a chain of *fast-lube-type* service centers that collect and recycle all the used motor oils resulting from its activities, and another to a chain of department stores that does not collect any used oils from its customers. If the law in the jurisdiction in which the company operates does not require an oil producer to ensure that its wholesale customers reclaim waste oil, and the producer's environmental policy is to do the minimum required by law, then a decision by the producer to not require its customers to collect waste oil might go unchallenged by an ISO 14001 auditor. However, the producer, in conforming with Section 4.3.1 — Environmental Aspects, of the ISO standard, would have identified 'ultimate disposal of the waste automotive oil' as a significant aspect of its activities and would have considered the impacts in the process of setting its environmental objectives. It is reasonable to assume that in a situation as blatantly obvious as this (i.e., any environmental professional with any experience at all in dealing with waste automotive oils knows if no convenient provision for its disposal is made available to consumers, that it will wind up in landfills, backyards, and storm drains), the company would be expected by an auditor to have taken some action to address this aspect of its operation.

Having presented the 'reasonable' assumption in the preceding paragraph, it is important to note that its reasonableness is a subjective call, and this subjectiveness calls into question the credibility of the standard. Section 5.3.3 — Assignment for a Specific Registration, of the NAP, provides a mitigating factor with respect to this concern: "the registration body shall ensure that the skills brought to each [audit] assignment ... have appropriate technical knowledge of the specific activities for which registration is sought and, where relevant, with associated procedures and their potential for failure." This suggests that qualitative factors are to be considered in an EMS audit.

Although the example discusses voluntary environmental performance beyond what is required by regulation, the issue of credibility is very important to all stakeholder sectors because the promise of superior performance is a major attraction for the federal and state environmental agencies, is potentially the only attraction for environmental advocacy groups, and is the private-sector's premier bargaining chip in its negotiations for alternative compliance assurance programs.

If the same company decides to manage its environmental aspects at a much higher level of performance, it may determine that the ultimate fate issue requires action. In the example given, the *fast-lube* customer collects and recycles all its waste oil. The producer may determine that this action is consistent with its environmental policy and nothing more remains to be done. The producer then needs to decide how to address the no-return policy of its department store customer. Section 4.3.1 of ISO 14001, states that "the organization shall ... identify the environmental aspects ... over which it can control and over which it can be expected to have an influence ..." Such influence varies among different situations, customers, and suppliers. The oil producer may be able to influence the department store chain to take back used oil. As an alternative, the producer may ask the chain to set up its own EMS as a condition of doing business. In this case, the producer is essentially asking its customer to assume environmental responsibility for its actions, thereby providing a reasonable justification for exclusion of the department store operation from the bounded area of the producer's environmental responsibility. The producer may also be capable of exerting influence across a particular industry, and such influence may result in the establishment of an *accepted practice* regarding this aspect of environmental responsibility.

Drawing the Box

The process by which an industry defines the boundaries of its environmental responsibility will remain subjective until enough *'boxes'* are drawn that *accepted practices* become established. This suggests that development of self-policing environmental management systems should involve a series of steps, each with a *'shake-out'* period sufficient to establish new *standard practices* based on a new set of commonly held *'meanings'* among stakeholders — i.e., a new social reality or *reality platform.*

In the example of the motor oil producer, a situation is described in which an obvious environmental impact might have been overlooked by the organization and caught by its auditor. It raises the question, "To what extent is it the responsibility of the auditor to determine where the company defines the boundary of its responsibility?" While it is true that an EMS audit team must have appropriate environmental expertise, no clear instruction appears to exist regarding this qualitative aspect of the audit. It is the responsibility of the organization to make this determination. This is an area of discomfort for some agency and NGO representatives who view environmental performance *beyond* regulatory requirements as the only justification for accepting ISO 14001 certification as an appropriate credential for preferential regulatory treatment. How can they be assured that an auditor will be rigorously discriminating in assessing the appropriateness of the boundaries of environmental responsibility delineated by the company, and not only the adequacy of the activities that occur within them? Again, the pursuit of an answer logically leads back to the need for a generally accepted definition of *accepted practice.*

The Yorktown Refinery case study provides an example of how the ISO 14001 system could provide environmental benefits beyond what is required by law. Although now in compliance with applicable regulations governing the release of benzene from one of its operations, this AMOCO facility still releases a significant amount of the pollutant from unregulated sources. AMOCO offered to eliminate this pollutant source instead of a smaller regulated source because it could be done less expensively. EPA found that, in spite of the obvious environmental benefit of eliminating the larger source, it did not have the authority to grant this substitution.[121] Under the ISO 14001, however, AMOCO would clearly have had to identify the unregulated release as a significant environmental aspect of its operations. Then, depending upon its policy, remediation may have been warranted.

This example raises the question: "What is it that we are trying to accomplish with our system of environmental regulations, and is it relevant today?" The concern is explained by a developer of the ISO 14000 Standards:

> Okay fine, you've gotten these companies to be in compliance with the law. Good. Does the law really cover all environmental aspects of that enterprise? — Number one. Number two, you've got these companies to be in compliance because these companies are smart, they've hired a bunch of people, said 'okay you guys, you keep us in compliance with the law.' These guys are good enough, they're technical enough that they can actually make the organization be in compliance. They figure out how to be in compliance. The rest of the organization doesn't know diddly-squat about environment. The rest of the organization, they have not developed an environmental culture, they have not developed an environmental ethic. The reason that companies are in compliance with the law is because of the heroic efforts of a few individuals who go around making sure that the dike doesn't break. That's what it is. Is that what we want? ... Did we not want to establish an environmental culture in this country? Didn't we want to get all the people involved? ... I mean, that's the way, the sustainable way to get everybody behind the environmental

> ethic and the environmental concept. And how have we done that? We haven't done that. Okay, so, we can talk about all the great achievements of the regulators, but in point of fact, the only achievement is that we've got some companies to be in compliance with the laws. Have we accomplished, really, what we wanted to accomplish? I don't think so (ISO).

ISO 14001 requires every employee whose work creates a significant impact upon the environment to be aware of the impact, competent, and trained to manage it appropriately. By comparison,

> ... in the current situation you have specialized functions in organizations that do environmental protection and the rest of the organization goes about doing its own business... . The 14000 will create an environmental ethic, will create — if done right — an environmental culture in organizations which is of inestimable value (ISO).

An interesting, though somewhat tangential philosophical conundrum regarding compliance and environmental policy-making under ISO 14001 is, if ISO 14001 requires compliance with all applicable environmental regulatory law as a mandatory minimum goal, what are the expectations for a company (e.g., AMOCO) that has a pollutant discharge that exceeds regulatory standards for environmental protection, but because of a statutory loophole is not regulated?

Concerns Over the ISO 14001

"Although they make a commitment to compliance on paper, they could devote almost no resources toward compliance or have a very elaborate compliance component to their system" (EPA).

Section 4.5.2 of the ISO 14001 standard is explicit in stating that "action taken to eliminate the causes of actual and potential non-conformances shall be appropriate to the magnitude of problems and commensurate with the environmental impact encountered." The focus is on continuously improving the environmental management system and procedures in order to bring the organization into conformance with its stated environmental goals — which at a minimum is regulatory compliance. Also, ISO requires that such actions and their corresponding results be documented. Conformance auditors will review such records in assessing an organization's environmental performance.

> So, the registrar comes around and says, 'you have a really good compliance system ... you had ten non-compliances of this severity and so on and so forth, but you have a process in place to address these non-compliances and to get yourself in shape. Fine, your EMS is good, I believe you, you get registered.' Come back a year later: 'Okay, let me take a look at your EMS again. Now tell me how many non-compliances have you got.' The guy says, 'Well, you know we tried our best, but we

> still have the same number of non-compliances and the severity is just as bad.' The registrar at this point says '... your EMS is not good enough... . we're not going to register you. You can't get registered. There is no registration.' The requirement of the system is that you improve your EMS continuously to handle the situations that you have. If your situation is not improving ... then your EMS is not working' (ISO).

Debates about commitment to regulatory compliance often are commingled with those about commitment to environmental performance beyond compliance. The link is, as stated earlier, that portions of both private and public sectors view the latter as collateral to be used to purchase flexibility to achieve the former. It may be necessary to separate the two levels of commitment in order to accurately consider the costs and benefits associated with each.

Will the ISO 14001 EMS certification be legitimate and credible? Strong consensus of opinion exists reaching across every sector that environmental management systems in general, and the ISO 14001 in particular, are likely to produce superior environmental performance: "The key to good environmental performance is management systems. The premise is sound" (NGO). Generally, it is recognized that an organization's commitment to establish an EMS is itself a commitment to the environment: "A firm that would go through the efforts of a management system audit ... is less likely to have environmental incidences" (SG). This recognition goes a long way to mitigate the concerns about legitimacy. Increased efficiency and effectiveness associated with better organization rank high on the list of benefits associated with an EMS, followed by consistency and stability of operations, and creation of an environmental culture.

The concerns that do exist are principally associated with the credibility and integrity of the accreditation and registration process — "if it turns out to be a sham registration, you know, there's really not a lot of credit that we can provide" (EPA) — and the qualifications of the registrars. However, expectations regarding registrar performance do not appear to be overly unrealistic. Clearly, performance measurement and commitment to quantifiable results are viewed as important components.

Can a company trust itself to live up to its own promises? Consistency of environmental commitment across an individual organization is a concern of corporate environmental managers in organizations moving toward increased voluntary performance. New top-down policies and directions are often not enough to convince employees that a change is warranted and consequently, performance in support of new initiatives may be sporadic or unreliable. New meanings need to be internalized by employees before they can be expected to engage reliably in the new desired actions. As much as it is clear that the private-sector is now seeking more control over how it meets its environmental commitments, there is some apprehension among some private sector managers concerning the viability of doing so. Without the threat of fines, fees, penalties, and incarceration, the environmental manager is ill-equipped to single-handedly enhance environmental performance. Of course the threats still exist for those aspects covered by regulatory law, but for voluntary action beyond compliance requires a belief system that values the environment and connects individual activity to it. So, while one of the promises of ISO 14001 is that it will bring about a culture of enhanced environmental awareness, conversely, the cultural shift will have to begin before it is likely to deliver superior environmental performance.

Recognized internal and external legitimacy of the voluntary EMS thus may be as important an issue for private-sector environmental managers as command-and-control authority is for agency regulators, because without the prominence it brings, they may find it difficult, if not impossible, to induce their colleagues to embrace environmental performance as part of their own realities.

Preferential Treatment

In 1970, based on a very limited core of information, this nation created a command-and-control, enforcement-based policy to deal with the environmental problems society was facing at that time.[122] Industry was identified as a principal target. Many believe that this policy is now outdated and needs to be revised. On March 16, 1995, President Clinton announced a plan for reinventing environmental regulation[123] asserting that "EPA is hobbled by overly prescriptive statutes," and recommending that EPA grant more responsibility to environmental stakeholders. Industries that have adopted progressive environmental policies and implemented productive environmental management systems expect to be treated as responsible corporate citizens. Some attempts are being made to elevate the status of such organizations with respect to environmental regulatory programs.

> We've got to change the culture again. It took us 20 years to change culture from 1970 to 1990. Now we need to change the culture again.... The first time around, the public and the environmental agencies said yes, we've got to have a clean environment and it took time to change the culture of industry. Now what has happened is that you sort of have the converse there, what you have is industry saying, 'We want to be recognized for outstanding achievement' (SG).

Elevated status makes sense to many regulators who would rather reduce the time they spend looking at good performers in order to spend more time with those that are problematic.

> The worse you are the more scrutiny you get, and ... if we believe a company is performing and going above and beyond the call of duty ... we'll spend less time paying attention to them. So, we could reduce or simplify, or streamline reporting requirements; possibly reduce, streamline or allow them to self-certify for permit applications, because we have some

> reason to believe that this is a proactive company that is doing the right thing (EPA).

EPA Region 1 is attempting to establish preferential status through its Star Track program. Star Track establishes "a separate regulatory track for 'Stars' .... Companies under a variety of scenarios can be identified as being higher performers" (EPA). Elevated status can mean that a company receives preferential treatment in selection procedures for a variety of beneficial government programs. "One of the benefits of this enhanced regulatory track that you get if you're a good performer, is you get to be considered for other programs at the head of the pack" (EPA). Preferential selection for government contracts is another potential benefit that a company might receive if it earns elevated status; "government procurement is a very big area" (EPA) in which companies can potentially receive benefits in reward for outstanding environmental performance.

ISO 14001 certification may be adequate to provide regulatory agencies with assurance that a particular company is performing responsibly with respect to the environment. "ISO will stand in as shorthand for good behavior" (NGO). This opportunity is likely to become more meaningful to regulators as ISO is increasingly adopted, and the list of companies worthy of consideration for elevated status grows. Agencies will not have the resources to devote to detailed evaluations of, and negotiations with, companies that are good environmental performers in order to determine whether they should be treated as such. ISO 14001 certification is well positioned to provide this check for them.

> If a company has an environmental system in place that can demonstrate that it can get a company into compliance and keep it there in addition to the other goals and objectives that the company sets for itself and can be certified by a third party to be in conformance with all of that ... given that situation, plus probably given compliance history of that organization, could the regulators reasonably and with public trust and confidence say, 'I do not need to come in and inspect and have the same amount of paper work or the same number of inspections for that organizations in order to issue permits as I do for an organization that doesn't have that situation?' It seems like a very carefully and almost laboriously planned out scientific experiment, but I think for a while that is the way it will have to go (EPA).

Rites of Passage

The expression at the end of the last paragraph, "but I think for a while that is the way it will have to go," sheds some light on the process of change in a regulatory agency. Transitional steps can be important, and perhaps requisite, components of regulatory change. Regulators involved in implementing policy require means to ensure that no unintended consequences result from mid-course corrections or policy shifts. Policy makers need to identify and address the logistical implications of the new directions they set for their respective organizations.

Transition design can be as important as policy design, because lacking a viable transitional plan, it may be impossible to get support at the operations level if there exists a possibility that the integrity of the existing program will be corrupted by the change. This is apparent in the difficulty EPA is having in *reinventing* itself despite orders from the highest office for it to do so.

> Culture change is a big concern. Let's say our commissioner says we're going to jump right in and do 14000. You know that staff people can stop it, no matter who the commissioner is… . Culture change is very important so you need to bring people along … to get people to realize that there are alternative ways to getting there (SG).

One state agency recently faced resistance from its regulatory operatives who were instructed to implement a new partnership-type regulatory policy. The concern in this case focused specifically on the areas in which they were being told to disregard activities that they recognized as integral parts of their responsibility. The regulators were instructed to visit a number of facilities and to collaborate with the companies there that had voluntarily agreed to participate in a state-sponsored pollution prevention initiative. The regulators were perplexed by their instructions *not to issue* notices of violation for anything less than an egregious environmental problem or health risk. Senior agency officials had to go out to the regions to meet with these individuals and assure them that what they were being asked to do was consistent with the agency's mission and mandate.

This phenomena is not limited to government agencies, as evidenced by the following testimony of one corporate environmental manager:

> If the CEO of IBM says this is what we're going to do, then obviously IBM is going to do that — well that remains to be seen. Basically, the people in the corporation have to agree with their CEO if it's going to happen. If they don't agree … it's not going to happen. So, it doesn't really matter what a CEO says sometimes, okay, he may be sincere, but if you don't have a culture, if you don't have an environmental ethic, or — it doesn't have to be environment, it could be any subject — but if you don't have your troops behind you, it's not going to happen (ISO).

Fewer Inspections

Two things are clear regarding frequency of inspections. One is that there is agreement that it makes sense for regulators to spend less time inspecting good environmental performers than they do on those with lots of, or recurring, environmental problems. And two, there is already an informal system in place that recognizes good performers:

> If you've got a company that's had 10 years of good compliance and you send your various teams out there and they say this is got a clean bill of health, just like going to a doctor you say, 'clean bill of health, see you in a few years' (SG).
>
> ... and it does have the boon of really freeing up a small number of resources that are being stretched very thinly at the moment, to go catch bad guys — which does need to be done (NGO).

Flexibility, speed, management autonomy, self-governance, reduced or eliminated permit requirements, elevated status, preferential treatment, reduced or deferred penalties of violations, and reduced paperwork constitute an impressive list of potential regulatory benefits for ISO 14001-certified organizations. It all appears possible and contingent upon the private-sector successfully demonstrating that it will be at least equally forthcoming, on a reliably continuous basis, with environmental benefits.

9

The Promise of ISO 14000

Still one thing more, fellow citizens — a wise and frugal government which shall restrain men from injuring one another, which shall leave them otherwise free to regulate their own pursuits of industry and improvement, and shall not take from the mouth of labor the bread it has earned. This is the sum of good government, and this is necessary to close the circle of our felicities.

— *Thomas Jefferson, 1801*

Inadequacies of EPA's Regulation of the Private-Sector

EPA's current system for regulating the private-sector ("*the system*") is perceived as onerous, inefficient, inappropriate, heavy-handed, outdated, and inflexible. Deficiencies occur in two principal areas of concern: (1) *The system's* burdensome complexity; and (2) Its unwarranted compliance enforcement-orientation.

The system's silo-like approach to the protection of each of the environmental media without reasonable regard for the others creates a Kafkaesque and labyrinthine entanglement of rules, regulations, and policies that are impossible to follow without encountering irreconcilable conflicts. As a result, regulated organizations are unable to achieve 100 percent compliance and remain engaged in a continuous effort to accommodate *the system*. Such efforts dampen the enthusiasm of environmental managers, who typically are committed to protecting the environment, and consume resources that might otherwise be used to enhance environmental performance beyond that which is minimally required.

Attempts by EPA to work around *the system*, to assuage the frustration of individual organizations or industry groups facing regulatory conflicts, are likely to result in the promulgation of new situation-specific regulations that further convolute *the system* and make no sense when considered in instances and contexts of other specific situations.

EPA itself struggles to work within this system; a system not entirely of its own design. Agency officials, too, are frustrated by overly prescriptive enabling legislation. EPA's consequent inability to decisively redirect its own course of action results in internal turmoil and overall impotency with respect to its ability to respond to the nation's changing needs.

The system inappropriately focuses on compliance with regulation, rather than on environmental protection. The presumption is that if compliance is achieved, the environment will be protected. Seven faults are identified in this line of reasoning:

1. *The system* was designed and developed in an era characterized by rampant industrial pollution and an industrial sector that was indifferent to society's concerns about the environment. It was entirely appropriate at the time to concentrate on the gross and egregious instances of pollution and, in the interest of expediency, not to be overly concerned with optimal efficiency. Clear and strictly enforced commands directed regulated organizations what to do, and to a large extent how to do it. Today, the industrial sector is very much aware of society's concerns about the environment, and progressive companies are to an impressive degree committed to proactive efforts to protect it. The problem arises when attempts by industry to develop and implement more efficient and effective approaches to reducing pollution are blocked by the rigid structure of *the system.*

   EPA officials are not blind or insensitive to this conundrum and recognize the vulnerability of the Agency maintaining a position antithetical to its principal mission. While the Agency has declared its intention to refocus its efforts from compliance enforcement to pollution prevention, such efforts are hampered by its own internal rigidity, the specificity of some of its authorizing legislation, and its interest in avoiding legal action that can be brought against it by citizens acting under provisions of environmental laws entitling them to sue the Agency for failing to enforce the requirements of those laws. EPA's internal turbulence over this issue makes it obvious to the regulated private-sector that the outcome of attempting to negotiate alternative strategy with it will be unpredictable. As a consequence, some progressive companies have elected to forego opportunities to participate in EPA's most flexible programs for fear that the Agency would not be able to live up to its own commitment to such programs. Unfortunately, their fears have been confirmed by a succession of withdrawn proposals, stalled programs, and the well-publicized testimonies of exasperated industrial leaders and high-ranking state officials.
2. EPA's performance is evaluated quantitatively on the basis of how many notices of violation it issues and how much in fines it collects.

As the large egregious problems have been eliminated, regulators, in order to maintain the perception of consistent or increased productivity, have been driven to issue notices of violation for more numerous and less significant problems. This unreasoned practice widens the relational gap between compliance enforcement and environmental protection. It is a particularly insidious problem because its self-sustaining tendency is to move the agency in a direction diametrically opposed to the logical outcome of an appropriate enforcement enterprise, which is for the number of violations to diminish.

Qualitatively, it is clear that this method of evaluating *the system's* performance is invalid and works against voluntary private-sector efforts that go beyond regulatory compliance because they are not associated with violations of regulatory law. To the extent that EPA reallocates its staff resources away from compliance enforcement and to collaborative pollution prevention programs, it threatens its ability to justify its continued existence.

3. Even when there is a clear and strong association between compliance with an environmental regulatory law and protecting that portion of the environment to which it is dedicated, the fact remains that the direct motivation for the regulated organization is to comply with the law, not to exceed its requirement, and not to protect the environment. Additionally, environmental laws do not protect all aspects of the environment, only those specifically identified, and even then, only in certain situations and under specified conditions. Consequently, situations occur, like that at the Yorktown Refinery, where the environment suffers because *the system* forces the regulated community to comply with the letter of the law rather than with the intent.

   As long as EPA is divided on this issue and a strong proponent for rigid interpretation of the law remains, it is unlikely that the Agency will be willing to put itself in a position in which it might have to defend, in court, a decision based on its interpretation of the intent of a law which conflicts with a requirement specified in its text.

4. Environmental management is segregated from other aspects of business management because of the exceedingly specific and prescriptive nature of its operation. The regulated community is required to conform to the agency's standard formats and procedures. While this approach provides a level of comfort for regulatory reviewers, it almost guarantees that systems established in regulated organizations for managing environmental compliance will not match up with the systems in place at those very same organizations for managing other aspects of their business

operations. Environmental management systems designed primarily to respond to the dictates of *the system* are understandably alien to the managers of other departments. The problem introduced to a business organization by this situation is that relevant information is not shared. Symptomatic to the problem are three related concerns:

1) Lack of common knowledge, procedures, and management systems means that staff and data management resources are difficult to share between the environmental management departments and others.
2) The operationally isolated environmental management department is more vulnerable to upsets by turnover in personnel because a disproportionately large share of the knowledge base leaves with the individual.
3) The lack of shared knowledge represses employee *ownership* of environmental problems. As a result environmental consciousness and culture remain uncultivated, and environmental compliance assurance continues to require a greater effort on the part of the organization's environmental managers than would otherwise be the case.

5. Economic and environmental sustainability are not fundamental components of *the system.* While waste reduction is at the top of the EPA's environmental management hierarchy, the vision stops far short of a sustainable future and consequently, it is not viable for the long term. In view of the world's growing population, shrinking resources, and increasingly stressed environment, such short-sightedness can mean that even the most well-intentioned efforts to protect the environment, as that task is defined today, may be wasting resources that could be used more optimally to provide a sustainable future.
6. As pollution control activities have migrated upstream in the process from the end of the discharge pipe to the production floor, agency expertise has become less relevant in the effort to reduce pollution. The knowledge required to design and implement in-process enhancements is industry-specific and it is within industry only that such knowledge can be reasonably expected to exist. Agency control of, or influence over, production processes can be expected to result only in economic inefficiencies.
7. An increasingly competitive global marketplace requires U.S. industry to be more responsive to changing market demands. *The system's* sluggish review and approval processes for regulatory permits and permit modifications reduce industry's responsiveness and threaten the nation's economic vitality and viability.

The Promise and Potential of ISO 14000

> *The highest and best form of efficiency is the spontaneous cooperation of a free people.*
>
> —*Woodrow Wilson, 1921*

Industry no longer ignores the regulated environmental aspects of its activities as it did a quarter of a century ago. Widespread adoption of the ISO 14000 Environmental Management Standards and certification under its ISO 14001 Environmental Management Systems specification now promises to expand the scope of industry's attention to include areas beyond minimum regulatory requirements, areas of non-regulated environmental concerns, and aspects of environmental activities over which it has influence but which, traditionally, have been considered beyond the borders of its responsibility.

Environmental managers now have credibility, resources, and authority within progressive companies. Environmental management policies and procedures influence how a company operates. ISO 14000 will expand this influence deeper into the organization to individuals in companies that would be otherwise uninvolved, and more broadly in society to other companies that regulatory agencies might never visit.

An ISO 14001-certified organization will, at a minimum, commit itself to regulatory compliance and establish an environmental management program to bring it into compliance. The objective of the system of checks and balances that define the 14001 standard and make it unique among other voluntary programs require the organization to:

1. Appropriately and adequately identify all environmental aspects of the operations and activities it controls and over which it can be expected to have influence.
2. Determine, in accordance with the level of commitment presented in its environmental policy statement, which aspects are significant or have the potential to have significant impacts.
3. Establish an environmental management system capable of addressing all significant aspects in a manner appropriate to their magnitude and nature, and consistent with all regulatory requirements and the organization's environmental policy.
4. Commit resources of the type, and in the amount necessary, to successfully implement its environmental management programs and to meet its objectives.
5. Design and implement a program to monitor and measure progress toward meeting its environmental objectives.

6. Conduct periodic environmental management system audits to assess the appropriateness and efficacy of the EMS and its activities.
7. Conduct periodic top-management reviews of the EMS, its progress, audit reports, and all other relevant data and determine the extent to which it is meeting its objectives.
8. Institute changes to the EMS to correct deficits uncovered during the review.

The premise is, if an ISO 14001 EMS is in place and certified, the organization, as a result, will have superior environmental performance. Interestingly, this is precisely the argument presented earlier as EPA's rationale for focusing on compliance enforcement rather than on pollution prevention. The differences between the two in this respect are significant:

- Regarding their development, ISO 14001 was developed between 1992 and 1996, by experts from across the globe with a wealth of experience developed over a 25-year history of managing environmental problems. It was approved in September 1996, and development continues on the other standards in the 14000 series that will serve as guidance documents for use with the EMS standard. The model for EPA's *system* was designed a quarter of a century ago, with limited knowledge and experience, and by a relatively few individuals with a very narrow focus.
- Regarding their processes, the EPA *system* keeps the regulated community one step removed from environmental concerns. The Agency evaluates the environmental aspects, then determines and specifies appropriate actions and levels of protection. The regulated organization then responds to these specified instructions. The ISO 14001 program requires the organization to evaluate its environmental aspects directly, and to determine what actions are appropriate. Regulatory requirements are minimally acceptable actions under ISO.

The purpose of ISO 14001 is to "provide organizations with the elements of an effective environmental management system … to assist organizations to achieve environmental and economic goals."[124] While regulatory compliance is not a stated purpose of the standard, its measurement, monitoring, documentation, and data management requirements provide an organization's management with the information that it needs to determine its progress toward environmental objectives. This will also provide regulators with a means to determine compliance status. ISO's audit requirements, generally acknowledged in the U.S. as a third-party function, adds credibility to the process. The availability of monitoring data, evaluations, and external verification will provide the agency with a credible means of checking on the compliance of an organization without having to perform an intrusive compliance inspection.

Other promises and potentials of the ISO 14001 include the following:

- It operates at the level of the individual. ISO 14001 requires organizations to establish and maintain verifiable procedures to make employees aware of the significance of the potential environmental impacts associated with their work, their responsibilities in managing those aspects, the importance of conformance with the organization's environmental policies, and to provide appropriate training to all personnel whose work may impact the environment.
- It provides a standardized EMS. Moving away from government-specified procedures and toward those that are organization-specific will impose added demands on regulatory agencies. Widespread acceptance and adoption of the ISO 14001 EMS standard will ease that transition by defining the foundational elements of the EMS and providing standardized third-party evaluations. Agency staff can thus become familiar with a common and internationally accepted model, and use this understanding as the basis for evaluating any voluntary EMS.
- It provides an EMS system with self-monitoring, self-policing, and self-correcting elements. Typically, EPA requires organizations that are interested in participating in its voluntary programs to have in place an EMS, a monitoring program, and a third-party audit mechanism. These elements all are requirements of the ISO 14001 standard.
- It satisfies U.S. commitment as a member of the World Trade Organization and the preference established in the National Technology Transfer Act to use international standards wherever possible. The ISO 14001 is the internationally accepted environmental management standard. Additionally, it was developed to be compatible with the ISO 9000 series of international quality standards.

Worldwide interest and participation in the ISO 14000 series and ISO 14001 certification has grown dramatically. In the U.S., all large manufacturing corporations involved in international trade are paying close attention to ISO 14000-related developments. Ford, AT&T Microelectronics (Lucent Technology), and 3M plan to register all domestic and international facilities to ISO 14001. Eastman Kodak plans on being "registration ready" within two years. U.S. corporations are currently considering ISO 14001 implementation at over 1,300 individual sites. In spite of the comments contained in a previous section of this work regarding IBM's hesitancy to commit to ISO 14001 registration, the electronics giant has announced its decision to seek registration for its entire operations worldwide.[125] The countries of the European Union unanimously adopted ISO 14001 as the EU standard within days of its approval. Japan's Ministry of International Trade and Industry is strongly encouraging their industries to become registered and certified under the standard, and the government of China has adopted ISO 14001 as state policy.[126] The ISO 14001 has clearly been adopted on a global scale and appears likely to continue to grow. ISO can be expected to grow qualitatively as well. Generally accepted practices and standard interpretations can be expected to develop as the number of implementations increase.

Process Not Project

What makes the ISO 14001 Environmental Management System standard unique among voluntary programs are its international acceptance, its third-party audit program, and the fact that it standardizes and codifies the basic elements for establishing an ongoing EMS process.

> First and foremost is that it can go on regardless of us.... Secondly, it's a systematic approach that lasts. When you put it in place it is an entire system, it doesn't stop at the end of a CSI [Common Sense Initiative] project or a Project XL. It actually, within an organization, establishes a flow of environmental responsibility throughout the entire organization (EPA).

Most voluntary environmental programs initiated by EPA require participating organizations to have an environmental management system, plus additional safeguards in place as a base from which to run specific Agency pilot programs like its Environmental Leadership Program, Star Track, and Merit Partnership.

> These pilots ... all require an EMS ... with other requirements such as pollution prevention audits, disclosure of environmental results, a pledge to promptly correct any violations (EPA).

To varying degrees, these latter elements all are requisite components of the ISO 14001 EMS. ISO 14001 provides the management system from which to run these projects, monitor their progress, make appropriate adjustments, and report their results. Of course, the ISO 14001 EMS is certainly not limited only to the management of government programs.

The preceding discussion illustrates how the ISO 14001 EMS can serve as an operational platform from which environmental enhancement projects are managed. Consistent with this description of its function, the preponderance of evidence leads to an understanding that at this point in time, it is not the act of adopting ISO 14001 that is likely to result in a company receiving regulatory relief, but rather the positive results of employing it to achieve an organization's enhanced environmental performance objectives. The positive results that accrue will become the collateral that will have value in negotiating for regulatory benefits.

Good-bye Charlie

At the present time, small pockets of expertise manage the vast majority of an organization's environmental aspects. The ISO program will be instrumental in effecting a shift toward organization-wide environmental responsibility:

> The shift for private industry is away from 'Charlie' who is always the head of EH&S in an organization. The CEO says, 'Charlie, I've given you an office, a nice salary, a phone, staff, you keep us out of trouble and I don't want to see you again.' And Charlie says, 'okay.' Now [under ISO 14001] ... the operational head of any organization is where environmental responsibility begins and everybody from the secretaries to the operational guys to the salesman to the budget people to the janitors of an organization know where they are in terms of the whole environmental policy and goals and objectives of an organization (EPA).

The role of the environmental manager in an ISO 14001 company becomes oversight, coordination, evaluation, and provision of expertise and specialized resources to employees across the organization. "So it's a whole shift in how they do things. CSI and XL don't have that broad of an impact over an Organization" (EPA).

Accepted Worldwide and It's Working

Probably the most unique aspects of the ISO 14001 standard are it international ownership and widespread adoption. "This isn't just an EPA program, this is a worldwide, internationally recognized program" (NGO). The International Organization for Standardization is well established and recognized in world trade, and its 'ISO' signature on this standard bring credibility to it. "It's got that sort of transferability aspect that obviously EPA's programs aren't going to" (NGO). Adding to its global acceptance is its compatibility with the ISO 9000 quality standards. This acceptance is evidenced by the dramatic and internationally widespread adoption of the ISO 14001 EMS since its approval in September 1996. "From what I hear, the thing that ISO's got on EPA's programs is that it's actually going somewhere. XL has kind of gotten stalled and lot of people are unhappy with Common Sense, etc." (NGO).

ISO 14001 as the 'Sanctioned' Environmental Management System

A Fait Accompli?

In the late 1980s, EPA proposed establishing a performance-based standard for landfill design. The proposal was resisted by solid waste management

(SWM) professionals who favored a menu of uniform, technology-based design standards. SWM professionals felt that the uniform standards would be preferable because they would be pre-approved by the agency. They believed it unlikely that the economic benefit of a site-specific design would outweigh the additional costs associated with the effort necessary to convince the Agency that the design would perform to its satisfaction. Following a parallel course of reasoning, the ISO 14001 may become the government-sanctioned EMS.

Environmental management systems are recognized as valuable components of an organization's business management infrastructure and federal and state agencies are increasingly requiring their contractors to have environmental management systems in-place, or recommending that they do. ISO 14001 is the international voluntary standard and its verifiable self-monitoring and self-policing aspects make it an obvious choice to consider. "Governments aren't going to have any other course but to adopt it" (IEM). There really isn't any other program to compete with it at this time. "I would bet against any other standard for a couple of reasons. First of all, ISO is worldwide. Second of all there is a huge momentum, huge inertia behind it" (NGO).

Regardless of how obvious a choice it may or may not be, most agencies are not prepared to identify it as the only EMS they will recognize. Some agency officials see it as only likely for large organizations, and are concerned about the cost of implementing the ISO 14001 system and the burden that requiring it may put on small and medium size businesses. Others see it becoming a familiar enough option that companies that implement it will be able to avoid considerable bureaucratic process in getting it recognized.

Certain industry groups, like the auto industry, are already moving aggressively to adopt ISO 14001, and are considering making it mandatory for its major suppliers. Many large organizations have committed to becoming 'registration ready' within a specified amount of time, typically 2 years, with the understanding that doing so is just good business management practice and when the time comes that the benefits associated with becoming certified justify the costs, they will act.

Developers of ISO 14001 and private-sector organizations committed to that development, are keeping a wary eye on government interest in the standard. The concerns are that EPA will require it on top of existing regulatory mandates and that the Agency may attempt to rewrite it as a performance standard focusing on outcomes rather than inputs.

> Industry is trying to keep EPA from making it [ISO] mandatory, unless there is some benefit ... to being certified. Right now there isn't a particular driver to be registered and adopt that as your management system with EPA or even DEC, because they can't offer you anything in regards to it. So there is no hold in that regard (IEM).

> Finally, the U.S. has some responsibility under the National Technology Transfer Act and as a member of the World Trade Organization to adopt

international voluntary standards whenever possible. While this responsibility is not a mandate, it does give a very strong preference for the use of international standards and "if a dispute was brought against the U.S. government as to why we didn't use the internationally used standard, we would probably not be able to hold that up in a dispute court" (EPA).

The Inevitability of Change

A society always moving forward along the uncertain path of discovery should also recognize that most frequently it is the successes that generate the problems, because successes give you choices. There's an old saying that today's problems come from yesterday's solutions.

— Neal F. Lane, Director, NSF, April 22, 1997

This work reveals that in spite of their differences, considerable agreement exists among environmental professionals in industry, government, and nongovernmental organizations, regarding problems with the current system of regulation, the need for more responsibility at the level of the individual, and the desirability of the private-sector taking on more responsibility for protecting the environment. Changes are necessary in order to keep the U.S. economy strong, continue to improve the quality of the environment, and move towards a sustainable future. EPA is aware of the problems and acknowledges the needs, but faces enormous inertial and external forces and has been unable to change its bottom-line regulatory strategies to respond effectively and comprehensively.

EPA's strategy to reinvent itself by partnering with regulated organizations are often frustrated because they are based on the erroneous belief that true partnership can exist when one partner holds all the authority. In spite of the agency's insistence that it will give equal weight to the inputs of the various stakeholders, the fact remains that EPA can, and has *pulled the plug* on such efforts when negotiations began heading in directions that were uncomfortable for the agency. Moreover, EPA is attempting to form partnerships in the area of voluntary performance, i.e., performance beyond regulatory requirements. Such performance is beyond EPA's purview and the agency's quid pro quo contribution to the partnership, in compensation for the organization's superior environmental performance, has been little more than the bestowal of accolades and awards upon its partners. Such recognition has value and can be an effective motivator, but private-sector investment in initiatives that do not have a reasonable and measurable return on investment are typically commensurate only with a perceived value of that recognition. EPA has offered more substantial compensation in the form of regulatory flexibility, but internal inconsistencies and external pressures have prevented or minimized its capabilities in this area.

Independent of EPA's efforts, the International Organization for Standardization, responding to a request from the Earth Summit Committee in Rio de Janeiro, set about developing international standards for environmental management. The significant consequences of this act was the assemblage of a technical advisory group of environmental experts from over 65 countries around the world, the consequent development of the ISO 14000 International Environmental Management series of standards, and in September 1996, approval of the ISO 14001 Environmental Management System standard.

The ISO 14001 EMS stands alone in its qualifications and widespread acceptance, and provides a systematic, measurable, and verifiable means of placing the appropriate management of the environmental aspects of an organization's activities within the province of its responsibility. Compatible with the ISO 9000 series of international quality standards, the 14000 is expected to follow and surpass its pattern of widespread international adoption within 5 years.[127] Worldwide, tens of thousands of organizations are expected to implement various aspects of the ISO 14000 standards over the next decade.[128]

Clearly, the world has adopted the ISO 14001 EMS as its environmental standard. U.S. organizations should anticipate increasing pressure to conform to some aspect of the standard over the next 5 years. This will be so regardless of whether or not it satisfies any portion of EPA's regulatory compliance system. Furthermore, it is anticipated that the more ISO 14001-certified companies there are, the more proposals for innovative compliance alternatives EPA will have to review. The agency will either have to find ways to accommodate those that are worthy, or attempt to defend the unenviable position of preventing superior environmental performance in order to maintain strict regulatory compliance. This is not a tenable position for an agency dedicated to protection of the environment.

EPA's system for regulating industry was the right choice for the problems of the past. Its success has ensured its longevity, but the system is an inappropriate choice for the present and it is time for new choices.

ISO 14000: A Catalyst for Reinventing EPA

This work identified, evaluated, and compared the known inadequacies of the current system for the environmental regulation of industry as administered by the Environmental Protection Agency and its delegates, to the potentials of voluntary, private-sector environmental performance, specifically as prescribed by the ISO 14001 Environmental Management System Standard and other guidance documents in the ISO 14000 series. Manifold and multilayered relationships are revealed and strong correlations shown to exist between the needs of the one and the provisions of the other. Evidence abounds to demonstrate the deficiencies in the current system and an increasingly thick portfolio of successes documents the efficacy of the voluntary effort.

While perspectives vary across the sectors of society, clearly significant areas of consensus exist, particularly with respect to the inadequacies of the current system. EPA has attempted to revise its strategy for regulating industry to coincide with current needs and realities, and to make a cultural shift from that of an enforcement agency to that of an organization devoted to waste prevention. In spite of top-down directives from the nation's highest office, EPA has been unable comprehensively to make this shift. Clearly, the inertia of a quarter-of-a-century of command-and-control, enforcement-based regulatory strategy makes dramatic course corrections exceedingly difficult. Obviously, the levels of complexity both technologically and culturally associated with waste prevention are orders of magnitude greater than are those associated with end-of-the-pipe capture and treatment. Clearly, EPA lacks the resources necessary to adequately and appropriately manage the added burden of this complicated reality.

Greater variation exists among concerns regarding the promises and potential of voluntary private-sector environmental performance. Clearly, the principal private-sector concerns have more to do with profit than with prevention, and more to do with competition than conservation. Yet, the theories underlying the concepts of voluntary, private-sector environmental management systems and voluntary environmental performance, for the most part, tend not to be the areas of contention. A strong consensus does exist that significant value is added value when an organization establishes a comprehensive and systematic environmental management system with adequate monitoring and measuring sub-systems, a program of checks and balances including third-party audits and periodic review by committed top-level executives, and mechanisms for continuous improvement. Concern then focuses on the willingness of the private-sector organizations to make good the promise of the ISO 14000. Such credibility will have to be earned.

Implementation of ISO 14000 will occur regardless of government action. It will continue to grow because of its worldwide acceptance and ownership. This global phenomenon is spreading across national boundaries through commercial pathways and may only be slowed or hastened by government actions. Clearly, as voluntary environmental commitments are made, for whatever motive, the action that results from the commitment becomes part of the reality that defines the culture. Consistent with the symbolic interactionistic model that provides the means of interpreting this data, this elevated level of environmental performance thus provides a higher platform from which to survey the surroundings, gather information, and make decisions about the future.

Since, in the U.S., conformance with the ISO standards does not relieve an organization of its obligation to comply with environmental regulatory law, successes under the voluntary standard will accrue to its credit while failures are likely to be charged against the many roadblocks of the regulatory system. In this sense, the growth of the ISO 14000 membership will create increasing pressure on government for reform, and build public confidence in the efficacy and reliability of voluntary environmental management systems.

The significant correlation between the inadequacies of the current regulatory system and the provisions of the voluntary environmental management system ensures that the noted presence of one will illuminate the existence of the other. And, that unrelenting illumination will catalyze the reinvention reaction for EPA.

Section III

Preparing for the 21st Century

10

A Model for Change

If you should put even a little on a little, and should do this often, soon this too would become big.

— Hesiod, 700 BC

A Model for Regulatory Change

Most environmental professionals have not developed a distinct vision of environmental management in the distant future. They seek better paths on which to travel rather than a desired ultimate destination. It is possible to assess this approach alternately as short-sighted or as pragmatic. Most likely, it is a little of both.

The ability of an individual to envision a distant future may be assessed, in part, as a function of the height of the *platform* upon which she or he stands. For example, it is more likely that someone working in a progressive organization with a strong commitment to the environment (i.e., a relatively high *platform*) would be able to envision a production system with zero emissions or a sustainable economy than would an employee working in a particularly dirty industry that takes little or no preventative measures to protect the environment (i.e., a very low *platform*). The *platform* that exists in one situation provides a supporting *social reality* from which an individual can envision a range of possible futures that are different from those that can be envisioned from the vantage point of another.

Continuing with the *platform* metaphor, two preconditions to inducing change are identified: (1) the individual must be standing on a *reality platform* that supports a reasonable view of the location to which movement is desired; and (2) there must exist a means of getting the individual to look in the 'right' direction. Applied to regulatory change, and particularly from the perspective of the regulatory operative (as distinguished from the regulatory policy maker), there may be a third qualifying factor, a *transitional bridge.*

Literally translated as meaning 'transition design' or 'transition plan,' the *transitional bridge* provides the regulatory operative with some sense of assurance that what is good, right, just, and appropriate about the program that she or he has invested time and effort into, will not be lost, corrupted, or diminished as an unintended consequence of the change. The *bridge* may be a plan or procedure, or metaphorically speaking, a series of incrementally elevated *platforms* upon which to climb, one-at-a-time, and readjust one's sights. At each successive *platform*, the view ahead becomes clearer, while the view behind is not so far behind that it is lost, or the elements in it beyond control.

In view of the distrust and suspicion of the current social reality regarding the motives of the private-sector, it is unlikely that any plan for transferring environmental responsibility to the private-sector will be successful without three essential ingredients: (1) a guarantee that existing environmental quality standards will not be abandoned or diminished; (2) evidence that superior environmental performance will be achieved; and (3) assurance that the process for verifying voluntary environmental management performance is legitimate and credible.

Elements of Disparity

Two major elements of disparity among the sectors regarding what constitutes an appropriate and acceptable approach to the transference of responsibility from government to industry include the following:

1. **Degree of openness and control.** Currently, *the system* requires a regulated organization to provide information about its production process as well as about its treatment process and anticipated discharges as part of a pollution discharge permit application. The private-sector strongly favors modifying this requirement to eliminate the need for information about the production processes. Environmental organizations are adamant about the importance of keeping this information available to government and the community. Government favors an "open" approach as good public policy.

   A middle-of-the-road approach requiring the regulated organization to disclose process information as a condition of the permit, rather than as a prerequisite to it, appears to be gaining in popularity as a likely first step.

2. **Level of Performance.** In exchange for government providing more flexibility to regulated organizations, environmental NGOs want more than just compliance from the organizations and are looking for guarantees of superior environmental performance. Industry is willing to commit to superior performance as a goal, but is hesitant

to guarantee it. Government wants compliance at a minimum, but favors superior performance.

Considerable agreement among the three sectors asserts that an organization that has a good comprehensive environmental management system with an independent means of verifying its performance is likely to have superior results. Organizations with such systems in place are demonstrating that this is so. As the portfolio of successful EMS implementations grows, NGOs and industry are likely to grow more comfortable with the concerns and needs of the other.

A Precautionary Approach to Alternate Systems

Regulatory agencies will need to begin relying information from environmental management systems that are not their own. This may increase the likelihood of record-keeping error for the agencies but it will make industry systems more robust because they will thus be able to integrate their environmental management systems with their other business management systems. No longer will separate systems need to be maintained.

A precautionary approach can be taken to resolve the dilemma of where to locate the robustness. This involves examining the outcomes of a system failure under two different scenarios. If an industry's EMS fails, clearly it is likely that the environment will be impacted; this, after all, is where the pollution exists and is being controlled. If a system fails at a regulatory agency, an environmental impact will occur only if the industry's system fails as well, or if the industry, being aware of the agency's failure, decides maliciously and illegally to take advantage of the situation. It appears clear that if industry can be trusted, it is there that the maximum control should reside.

11

Factors Influencing Movement Toward a More Optimal Balance

However gradual may be the growth of confidence, that of credit requires still more time to arrive at maturity.

— Benjamin Disraeli, 1867

The Pace of Change

It appears that at some point in the early 1990s, a critical mass was reached relative to society's intent to change its approach to environmental protection. Considering the global proportions of recent efforts to encourage and codify voluntary, private-sector environmental performance, the swiftness at which agreements are being reached is breathtaking for many who are involved, and a concern for some.

> I think we really need some time to catch our breath. Everyone does, government, people who have developed the standards, to step back and really take a look at what these standards can and can't do in improving performance (EPA).

> The pace is unbelievably rapid… . It's hard for us to keep up … so we're trying to run as quick as we can, but even some of the more progressive states than we are in ISO 14000, are still having a hard time catching the train (SG).

Agencies may fear that they will lose control, or that they will have to face charges from the environmental activist community that government is attempting to roll-back 25 years of environmental regulatory development:

> Public trust is a big issue. The polluters in the United States have been business and industry. The federal government has been too; the DOD is a huge polluter. So, the public is leery of doing anything that looks too cooperative. In the U.S., we're still sort of a John Wayne society in many ways. So to move too quickly towards a real shift in the way we do things

> is going to be very suspect and I think that that is fine, it's probably a very rational thing to move slowly. But in this shift, you have to watch carefully, your public trust barometer (EPA).

Yet, industry too represents a legitimate constituency of government, and it is petitioning the agencies to keep up with a process that is being proffered as indispensable to the U.S. in maintaining economic competitiveness on the global market.

> We're running out here. We want you, government, to run as fast as us. We want you to learn total quality management. Not because we think it's good for government. We don't care if you guys fall on your face, but we know that if you don't master TQM, you can't get to us with speed, and speed is what we need to be competitive in our products in the marketplace. That's what they need. So the culture change has to be in government as well (SG).

Among some governmental officials who are committed to reinventing the environmental agency and involved in effecting a corresponding culture change, one concern is that they will not be able to keep pace with the global development. One official warned:

> [ISO] 9000 took several years to take off, but boy is it taking off now. The infrastructure is in place, the mindset is there, it's going to be a lot easier for people to make the connections and see the benefits. If they require their suppliers, which the 9000 certified are now requiring big time of their suppliers, it will happen that much more quickly with 14 [ISO 14000]. Instead of taking seven years, it's going to take two. And we'd better be ready, and we're not (SG).

NGO Involvement and Influence

Environmental advocacy organizations provide a valuable service to the agencies "as indicators of public trust ... If it looks like the regulators are going to give away too much, then they're going to scream and holler" (EPA). Until recently, these environmental organizations have paid little attention to the ISO 14000, partially because of the high costs of the worldwide travel involved in its development, and partially because initially it was not perceived as a truly relevant environmental concern.

> They [*the environmental NGOs*] had a chance to come into this process for five years. They came four years ago and they walked out again. They said, 'well this is management, we don't care about management, we help the government set performance standards, you guys can manage whatever you want to manage' and they walked out of the process. Now they're interested, now I get calls and they want to know — you know, 'send me copies of the standards, we want to study them.' Okay fine, alright. So now, you know, everybody has to come in at their own time I guess (ISO).

In spite of the recent interest, the number of NGO members who understand what ISO 14000 is about remains small. "Nobody really knows very much about ISO. It's only just starting to loom as an iceberg for people" (NGO). In spite of the slow start, the NGOs' wary response to other voluntary initiatives that have offered increased flexibility and transfer of environmental management responsibility to industry, like EPA's Project XL program, may well be indicative of what can be expected regarding ISO. "I think that that is appropriate, I think that it's going to be two steps forward and one step backward for a while" (EPA).

A Lesson Learned from Superfund

Superfund is a substantial motivator for the private-sector to initiate its own programs. Since so many large companies have been impacted by Superfund in one way or another, it can be viewed as more of a universally applied standard rather than as a punitive measure applied only to a few.

> The one big statute that has hit almost every big company at one point or another is Superfund. [and] ... since everybody is hit by Superfund, it's not as much of a system where we're catching violators, what we are catching is companies who in the past, disposed of their waste in a way that was not safe enough" (EPA).

Industry has learned through involvement with Superfund, that reliance on the letter of the law may not afford sufficient protection from environmental liability. "So that has created, in an ironic way, an enormous incentive for companies to deal with waste in a proactive, environmentally beneficial, safe way just to avoid Superfund liability" (EPA).

The Superfund liability threat is exacerbated by the fact that the federal government is not the only body that can initiate an action against a company for a cleanup:

> A private company could sue another with a Superfund claim, states have Superfund laws, and there's citizen suits. There so many players out there that can sue a company that violates, that there's incredible incentive to come into compliance" (EPA).

Developing Components

Before they are likely to bestow any regulatory benefits upon an ISO 14001-certified organization, agencies will need the environmental benefits associated with the adoption of the standard to be identified.

> IBM can't say and Kodak can't say, 'Oh, by the way we're now ISO 14000-certified so now give us relief.' We haven't educated ourselves yet in government to do that... . So it's going to be difficult in the early years to learn ISO 14000 [and say] 'yes, it solves the problem' (SG).

However, individual components of voluntary, private-sector environmental performance programs are being developed and demonstrated, and to the extent that they are successful, will serve to identify some of those benefits.

There are two areas in which voluntary, private-sector initiatives might satisfy agency needs, the first one being *due diligence*. The ISO 14001 specifications for developing and operating an EMS appear to coincide with EPA's due diligence criteria for eligibility for its audit policy benefits.[129] An EPA official involved in development of the Agency's environmental audit policy said, "My familiarity with the ISO 14001 suggests that it would satisfy the due diligence criteria described in the Audit Policy. These are the types of thing that a good EMS should be addressing" (EPA).

As defined in the Audit Policy,[130] "Due Diligence encompasses the regulated entity's systematic efforts, appropriate to the size and nature of its business, to prevent, detect and correct violations ..." As a point of comparison, ISO 14001 specifies that an organization's environmental policy be appropriate to the nature, scale, and environmental impacts of its activities (Section 4.2 (a)), that it take into account legislative requirements (Section 1, Scope), and that it include a commitment to comply with relevant environmental legislation and regulations (Section 4.2 (c)). In addition, ISO reaches well beyond regulated activities to include "those environmental aspects which the organization can control and over which it can be expected to have and influence (Section 1, Scope)." While a decision as to whether or not an organization will take action to mitigate impacts that reach beyond regulatory control will depend upon the environmental policy of that specific organization; commitment to compliance is a required element for all organizations certified under ISO 14001.

In order to qualify for benefits under the Audit Policy, an organization must establish compliance policies, standards, and procedures and assign responsibility for overseeing compliance. ISO 14001, Section 4.5.2, *Nonconformance and Corrective and Preventive Action,* states specifically that, "the organization shall establish and maintain procedures for defining responsibility and authority for handling and investigating nonconformance, taking action to mitigate any impacts caused and for initiating and completing corrective and preventive action."

The Audit Policy calls for "mechanisms for systematically assuring that compliance policies ... are being carried out, including monitoring and auditing systems." Correspondingly ISO 14001, Section 4.5.1, *Monitoring and Measurement,* requires establishment and maintenance of documented procedures to monitor and measure operations and activities that can have significant impacts on the environment. Section 4.5.4, *EMS Audits,* requires periodic EMS audits to determine if it is properly implemented and maintained, and Section 4.6, *Management Review,* requires top management review of the EMS and corresponding audit data to ensure continuing suitability, adequacy, and effectiveness.

Point for point, ISO provisions match EPA's Audit Policy requirements. The question is, therefore, should a company that is certified under ISO 14001 automatically be considered as exercising due diligence in managing its environmental aspects? And, if not, why not? This question lies at the very core of the topic being investigated and the scope of the discussion that follows extends beyond the specific instance of the Audit Policy. The answer, in part, will be a function of government's willingness and ability to rely on a system not of its own design. This issue is more complicated than it sounds at first. In spite of the variation that exists from one company to another, current regulatory procedures are fairly standardized. Up to now, the regulated community has been required to conform to the agency's standard formats and procedures. While this approach provides a level of comfort for regulatory reviewers, it almost guarantees that systems established in regulated organizations for managing environmental compliance will not match up with the systems in place at those very same organizations for managing other aspects of their business operations.

This situation tends to segregate environmental management from other business functions, and continues the practice of restricting environmental expertise to small groups of individuals. Herein lies a very important issue. One of the provisions of the ISO 14001 Standard that makes it attractive to industry is that is can help integrate an organization's environmental management system into its overall business management system. Consequently, it will not look so alien to managers from other departments and, as a direct result, this will enhance prospects for expanding environmental responsibility across the organization.

> Our [environmental management] systems may rely too much on individuals — and people leave — and our ability to maintain a certain level of performance is at risk when that happens ... if I can get the system strengthened, then it may be more robust and [then] even when people turn over, we don't backslide and lose so much ground ... and that's why I'm interested in it [i.e., the ISO 14001] (IEM).

The essence, then, of what is being considered here, is giving up standardization at the agency level in order to provide the opportunity for it to exist across an organization. The benefits would be manifold. The regulated organization could, as suggested earlier, develop a more robust environmental management system. It could combine its programs to address non-regulated environmental aspects with those that are regulated; this assumes that it would be unlikely for a company to set up a voluntary system to manage non-regulated aspects in a manner that mimics that of a regulatory agency for its own programs. Standardizing its internal management systems would increase the likelihood that an organization would engage in environmental activities beyond those required by law, simply because it would not entail a different system. And finally, overall efficiency would likely improve.

On the negative side, the agency program would become less robust, sharing responsibility would become more difficult, and overall efficiency would drop. In spite of these concerns, it already is widely recognized that the *one size fits all* approach is outdated and inappropriate and that the regulatory agency must change the way it does business. Also, it is clear that redirecting environmental management efforts from end-of-pipe to in-process will require increasing reliance on private-sector expertise.

Taking a precautionary approach to resolve the dilemma of where to locate the robustness, the outcomes of a system failure in each situation can be compared. If an industry's EMS fails, clearly there is a strong likelihood that there will be an environmental impact; this, after all, is where the pollution is being controlled. On the other hand, if a system fails at a regulatory agency, an environmental impact will occur only if the industry's system fails as well, or if the industry, being aware of the agency's failure, decides maliciously, and illegally, to take advantage of the situation. It appears clear, that if industry can be trusted, it is there that the maximum control should reside.

In order for government to change its approach, acknowledge progressive companies as innocent until proven guilty, and transfer responsibility for protecting the environment to them, it needs to present a defensible rationale to its environmental advocacy constituency. Of course, it can justifiably be argued that the ISO 14000 development committee itself is an environmental advocacy organization. Nevertheless, it is unlikely that a defensible approach can be planned without it containing several key ingredients, including: (1) a guarantee that existing environmental quality standards will not be abandoned or diminished; (2) evidence of demonstrated superior environmental performance; and (3) assurance that the ISO 14001 registration process is legitimate and credible.

The second area in which voluntary, private-sector initiatives might satisfy agency needs is *Design For the Environment* (DFE). DFE is an approach that could obviate the need for permits in many processes by eliminating all potential environmental insults. According to one state regulator, " we think ... that companies can even get out of the whole permitting requirements that they face now and all that that entails in hidden costs by having their operations from the get-go being more benign" (SG).

Generally, DFE is viewed as a third phase, or third generation, of environmental management enhancements. The first phase can be characterized as a *harvesting of the low-hanging fruit*, i.e., implementing actions that are easy to implement (e.g., turning off the water when its not in use, replacing lids on containers of volatile materials, general good housekeeping, etc.). Phase two involves enhancing existing products and processes, and includes actions like substituting benign materials for toxics wherever possible and modifying production processes to create closed-loop systems in order to extend the useful life of production materials and reduce or eliminate the generation of wastes and fugitive emissions. The DFE phase starts at conceptualization of a new product or service and considers the environmental aspects on a life-cycle basis.

DFE is a fairly new approach without a long history of demonstrated economic success. At this point it clearly makes sense to consider DFE for new products or new production lines — as opposed to redesigning those already in production.

> I think, in particular with regard to design for environment, it's mostly philosophy now, there's not a lot of tangible stuff available yet and I think that's going to change over the next five or ten years. And once you start getting some substance and once you start getting more global approaches to this and some more global commitment to this kind of approach, then I think that we'll start to see things happen (IEM).

Economic Influences

A decision whether or not to develop and implement alternative systems for environmental protection could be expected to depend ultimately upon some demonstrated answer to "the bottom line question of how can we get more efficiency out of our operations" (SG). It is not just an issue of whether or not a particular environmental enhancement will pay for itself. A decision maker must also consider how the return on the investment for the environmental project compares to other alternative investment opportunities.

The condition of the economy can influence the extent to which an organization is prepared to invest in environmental activities. Availability of funds is one concern:

> Things are easier to do and easier to implement when economic times are good. When economic times are bad, then you tend to pull back and hold back and wait for things to get better before you commit resources (IEM).

However, cutting one's overhead during difficult economic times is a traditional survival strategy and if the commodity market is slow, such times may in fact be favorable to internal environmental investments. Demonstrations of economic success *can* catch the attention of industry executives during periods of economic downturns when they might be expected to do only the minimum with respect to the environment.

Toward the end of the 1980s and into the 1990s, a few large companies in the vanguard of developing and implementing voluntary environmental management programs that targeted goals beyond environmental compliance, began reporting impressive profit gains realized through cost avoidance associated with reduced quantities and toxicity of waste being generated at their facilities. For example, in 1995, the Minnesota Mining and Manufacturing Company (3M) celebrated the 20th anniversary of its *Pollution Prevention Pays (3P)* program. 3M reported that during this time, it had initiated more than 4,000 pollution prevention projects, preventing the generation of 650,000 tons of pollutants[131] and saving the company $646 million,[132] demonstrating to other industries that environmental protection truly can pay.

Market pressure from large industrial purchasers of component parts from smaller manufacturers promises to play a major role in motivating small and medium size businesses to develop and implement verifiable voluntary environmental management programs. "Industry groups like the auto industry seem to be making a lot of noise about requiring to require all their suppliers to be registered. Well, that will drive a hell of a lot" (IEM).

Europe: Influencing Expectations

An increasingly global market exposes environmental professionals in U.S. corporations to environmental protection systems in place in other countries. Environmental managers in U.S. companies with multinational holdings frequently work with their non-U.S. counterparts managing parallel environmental aspects. Conditions are often reported to be more favorable outside the U.S., both for doing business and protecting the environment.

> Since I do a lot of traveling, I get to see relationships between government, industry and the general population in a lot of areas of the world. The U.S. is typically the one that I see in the worst light. Most other areas, Europe in particular, but not singularly, operate on the basis of partnership where there is a lot more trust between the three groups and a lot more interaction ... Europe is much less litigious, just to start with, so the idea of working together is kind of there in the first place [IEM].

> There is less of an adversarial relationship there [Europe]. Here if you go and ask for some kind of consideration or flexibility, their immediate assumption is, 'you're trying to pull the wool over my eyes' (IEM).

The elements of mutual trust and collaboration found in the European system are particularly attractive to U.S. environmental managers who have experience working there.

Citizen Lawsuits

Reported elsewhere in this work are charges that EPA does not have the legislative authority to act on its promise of providing regulatory flexibility for outstanding environmental performers. One stated concern is that even if EPA does choose to use its discretionary powers to not enforce a particular rule because it feels that the regulated company had already satisfied the intent of the rule through some alternative means, that company still might be forced to comply under a citizen lawsuit authorized under that rule. Consequently, even if the regulated community wanted to trust EPA to keep its promises, it knows that it may be a moot point. Some believe that legislative action may offer the only viable solution to this dilemma.

> The laws are there and laws don't go away unless they're changed. We've developed our system of laws around all the environmental factors, solid waste, water, air, etc. And they all generally have provisions for citizen lawsuits, so it encourages that level of activity and that whole thing is just well-ensconced and established. So innovative programs like XL, and Environmental Leadership Program from EPA are in deep tapioca right now (IEM).

A Political Issue

Progress toward environmental regulatory reform appears to have been partially derailed by an overly aggressive 104th Congress.

> The Republicans did their best to cause maximum mayhem in the situation in the last two years. They might have thought the time was right to try and do something, but I think they screwed it up royally and they've heightened the alert signals in the environmentalist community to an extent that didn't need to happen. Instead of drawing people into a partnership relationship, they alarmed everybody, including industry, I think. And it set the process back instead of plucking the fruit of regulatory reform that I think was really ready to happen. I think they single-handedly set it back and thought, 'now we're in charge,' which they weren't in the first place, because you could rule the Senate and the House, but there is a three-part government system here, checks and balances, and it just wasn't ready and the people weren't ready for it on the whole, not just the environmental groups (IEM).

In 1995, Congress under a Republican majority headed by a conservative faction, launched a major campaign to ease environmental regulation in the U.S. On July 28th of that year, House Majority Whip Tom DeLay (Republican-TX) asserted in the House of Representatives, that "the EPA, the Gestapo of government, pure and simple, has been one of the major clawhooks that the government has maintained on the backs of our constituents."[123] The campaign was described by Representative George Miller (Democrat-CA) as: "The most systematic and comprehensive assault on the environment and the environmental laws of this nation in the history of the country."[134] Public backlash against the Republican version of *regulatory reform* was considerable and most of the *reforms* failed when President Clinton vetoed the GOP's proposed budget[135] and when 40 Republican moderates refused to support an effort to override the President's veto.[136]

> Beginning in the heady days shortly after the Republican's 1994 landslide, a coalition led by a coterie of zealots sought to cut a third from EPA's budget, restrict its ability to enforce environmental laws and subject it to paralyzing procedural requirements ... The irony is that the zealots, in their helter-skelter rush to dismantle government, may have scuttled the most comprehensive effort to revamp EPA undertaken in its history.[137]

The ongoing efforts that may have been "scuttled" are the proposals set forth in the Clinton Administration's *National Performance Review.* Backlash against the Republican version of regulatory reform spread to Vice President Gore's "reinventing government" initiatives. As a result, concern about environmental regulatory reform has been heightened among environmental activists, and a certain amount of skittishness exists among those still seeking to support the reinvention plan, or who wish to propose constructive criticisms. George S. Hawkins, Esq., author of *The Eagle Agenda: An Agenda for the Future of Environmental Protection,* writes: "I argue that EPA can and should change. I run the risk of being identified with more crude and mean-spirited efforts to harm EPA — such is the consequence of the just-vanquished assault."[138] This author, too, has such concerns.

Understanding What Regulatory Relief Is Not

Notwithstanding the common understanding among those familiar with the ISO 14000 standards, that industry, in seeking regulatory relief in recognition of superior environmental performance associated with ISO 14001 certification, is not asking for relief from having to meet specified environmental quality standards, nor for the standards to be changed, concern still is warranted that such a misconception may play a role in generating opposition to the bestowal of this benefit upon worthy organizations. According to a developer of the ISO 14000 Standard,

> We're certainly not looking at reducing the levels of environmental protection. We're not looking at that. Regulatory flexibility doesn't mean deregulation. That's not what we're talking about (ISO).

Yet, it is not uncommon to hear environmental professionals who are not involved in evaluating ISO claiming that it means just that.

Reinventing EPA

In 1996 and 1997, environmental regulatory agencies in several states initiated progressive programmatic reforms in an effort to increase regulatory flexibility and develop partnerships with industry. Pennsylvania and Minnesota have done so in collaboration with EPA, developing pilot projects to evaluate voluntary private-sector programs like Project XL and ISO 14000 as alternative systems for protecting the environment. Some of these initiatives ran into trouble when EPA reportedly reneged on its promise to cooperatively support the efforts:

> One side of EPA is saying this is a good program, let's do it, everybody signs up, and all of a sudden [EPA's] Office of Compliance and Enforcement says we won't recognize any of those agreements that you people in EPA signed up for (IEM).

In late 1996 and early 1997, EPA took several very visible actions to warn progressive states that their authorizations to conduct federal programs and funding to support them could be withdrawn if they continued to move too quickly to transfer environmental responsibility to the private sector.[139,140] EPA's explanation for its recalcitrance was that "the Agency is concerned that a number of states and certain parts of the federal government might be giving too much credit to the ISO standard and what it can and can't do" (EPA). Industry's alternate explanation is that,

> Right now, EPA has absolutely no authority to provide flexibility ... Ultimately it came down to the compliance people in EPA saying, 'there is a law, you do the regulation based on law, you do benzene control at these emission points ... even though it's clear that the benefit, the payoff, is [better] the other way [i.e., cleaning up the unregulated releases]' (IEM).

This waffling on the part of the EPA sends a negative message to the regulated community regarding the likelihood that any efforts committed to voluntary environmental actions will result in regulatory benefits. It also alerts the community that in spite of any promises EPA might make regarding its willingness to collaborate in a venture that involves activities that will exist outside of its well-defined regulatory structure, the truth is that EPA might wind up using the access provided by such a collaboration to identify and take action on violations and areas of non-compliance.

Some more astute corporate observers recognized early on that in spite of the fact that President Clinton, in his March 16, 1995 *Reinventing Environmental Regulation* initiative, stated that the Project XL program is designed to give regulated sources the flexibility to develop alternative strategies that will replace or modify specific regulatory requirements on the condition that they produce greater environmental benefits, and notwithstanding his stated premise that the regulated "participants know better than the federal government how to reduce their pollution," it still was unlikely that EPA, acting under its authorizing legislation and the regulations promulgated thereunder, would be able to offer such a deal.

> One of the primary reasons that we didn't get into XL is our prediction that it would fail. Not because we didn't think it was a good idea, but because our question was, 'how are you going to get there' (IEM)?

ISO 14000 and EPA

It is clear that several issues relating to EPA's perception of the ISO 14000 standard require attention. One is the distinction between the comparative roles of environmental management systems and environmental compliance systems:

> [Some agency personnel] have been able to see the difference between … the management system and the compliance part… If you have a good management system, you're going to have good performance. You can't possibly help to do that. Whereas, other people, like in the Office of Compliance are saying, 'we won't trust that, no matter what, we won't trust it' and [cannot] imagine a system that is not linked, intricately linked to compliance (IEM).

Despite the clearly articulated intention of the international community not to turn the ISO 14000 into a performance standard, some agency personnel appear bent on doing just that. A 1996 letter from John Dombrowski in EPA's Office of Enforcement and Compliance Assurance (OECA), to Rosemary Maginnis at the American National Standards Institute (the U.S. representative body to ISO), requests ANSI's opinion regarding an EPA proposal to alter the ISO standard to include compliance assurance. Apparently this was proposed without even consulting the individual within OECA itself who was assigned to chair a task group to develop recommendations to the agency regarding the ISO 14001.

> (The task group chair) was shocked when he saw this, because he didn't even know it was being put together … What they did was, basically, rewrite ISO 14000. They've gone in and put in the things that they want to see there. There are a few deletions, you can see 'delete out' but the shaded are what they want to add… . This has the smacking of taking 14000 and doing to it what everybody didn't want to see happen, and that's building in strict command-and-control (IEM).

Another issue to be resolved is the need for a sound and widely acceptable definition of the term 'commitment to compliance,' as it is used with reference to the obligation of a company operating under an environmental management system conforming to the specifications set forth in ISO 14001. One side of the argument says that ISO 14001 does not require a company to be in compliance with environmental regulatory law and so ISO does not provide the assurance necessary to entrust private-sector participants with more environmental responsibility. The other side says that even a command-and-control, enforcement-based compliance inspection today won't ensure that a company is in compliance tomorrow and so it is capricious to demand this from the ISO standard.

Beans and the Paradox of Success

The method currently used by EPA to measure its success is problematic. An EPA official provides a lucid explanation:

> The biggest factor ... hampering ... moving [toward a more optimum balance of shared responsibility] ... is measurement ... What EPA has always been judged on is the number of ... enforcement actions that we do and the number of dollars that we bring in. It's all a basis of counting the numbers, or as we call it in government, beans ... And every year, a big 'to do' is how many enforcement cases we have, how many violations have we found, how many violation dollars have we collected. To me that's a crazy way to run an enforcement railroad. You hopefully wouldn't think that a police officer, or a police department, has done a better job because they have arrested more people or there have been more murder convictions if that means that there is more crime. When a police department does a good job, the number of crimes ought to fall. And unfortunately, we're under a system where we are constantly judged by finding a lot of violations every year. But to me, finding a lot of violations means a mistake and a problem, not a victory... (EPA).

EPA has a finite resource base. In order for it to devote more resources to partnership and collaboration for prevention, it must reduce what is allocated to enforcement. Consequently, enforcement numbers will fall. Additionally, as instances of gross pollution are eliminated, regulators, in order to keep the "bean" count high, are pressured into having to cite companies for less significant violations.

Standardizing Standardization

Regulatory agency officials were unanimous in stating that the agencies would be unlikely to specify the ISO 14001 as the only environmental management system that they would recognize as valid. Two reasons were cited for this. One was that some companies may have better systems already in place. Another was that small companies may not be able to afford the costs associated with ISO 14000 implementation and certification.

On the other hand, since the ISO standard is recognized as *the* international environmental management standard, it is likely to be the one that most regulators become familiar with, and may serve as a model for identifying appropriate EMS components and self-regulating protocol.

> One of the strengths of the ISO is to have one system that you can get to know well enough so that you don't have to reinvent the wheel or if you're a regulator here reviewing what someone's done, you don't have to understand a system that is of a construction that you've never seen before. There are distinct advantages to having a standard way [EPA].

And, the self-regulating aspect is one element of the ISO that will be difficult for other systems to duplicate. This is because of the rigorous process of authorizing the ISO 14000 registrars and certifying ISO 14000 auditors that participating organizations will rely on for demonstrating conformance with the standard and establishing credibility with their stakeholders.

If It Works, It Works

> I think over time, once the ISO registration process plays out, and government has gotten the information and has educated itself to a certain level, I think what will happen is, if we've got a process from 0 to 100 and somebody has ISO 14000 and they have other things that are going in their favor, they can go right to the middle — right to the head of the line, not all the way to the top, but right to the middle and cut out a lot of steps in between. But ... that is attached to ... commitment to results, measurable results. Those are the things that we really need to see. And if it works, it works. Practical solutions to practical problems (SG).

12

Environmental Responsibility in a Sustainable Society

Thinking is a momentary dismissal of irrelevancies.

— *Buckminster Fuller, 1969*

Some Things to Think About

Most environmental professionals have not given much thought to what life could, or should, be like in a society that has developed a sustainable relationship with its environment. Those who were asked for their opinions expressed surprise at being asked — "Wow! Interesting question — only because no one ever asks some of that at the staff level at EPA. Things like this are for the Washington think tank." They made it clear that their responses should be taken as spontaneous, rather than well-thought out: "You understand, of course, that this is off the top of my head." Yet a clear and common element of a future vision emerged from these spontaneous responses, a future in which environmental responsibility is much more shared than it is now:

> Citizens absolutely have got to get far more involved in these issues [and] no longer ... sit back and point at companies or other entities as ... the ones who are polluting' (EPA);
>
> ...equal responsibility [among government, industry and public] (NGO);
>
> ... everyone has a role (SG);
>
> ... individual responsibility that leads to corporate responsibility or industry responsibility (ISO).
>
> ... everybody takes environmental consideration into the fabric of what they do, how they operate a business, and how they run a family; how

> they run a school ... In that ideal then, communities are built of people who have this kind of inherent awareness. The need for environmental police is all but gone away ... maybe there will always be a need for some environmental enforcement (EPA).

As discussions of visions of the future lead to discussions of strategies for getting there, the role of the individual tends to become obscured by those of business and government organizations. However, the one essential thread discernible throughout is the assumption that there must be increased levels of individual awareness and responsibility. One recommendation is "that dispersing environmental responsibility to the smallest unit possible is the right way to go" (NGO). Perhaps this 'smallest unit' should be regarded always as the individual decision-maker.

> *It appears to me that ... the difficulties and disagreements, of which history is full, are mainly due to a very simple cause: namely to the attempt to answer questions, without first discovering precisely what question it is which you desire to answer.*
>
> —*George Edward Moore, 1903*

The question that needs asking is, "what do *we* as a nation want for the future regarding the environment?" It is apparent that a shared vision of the future — a set of commonly held meanings — is a likely prerequisite to increased individual responsibility. While "sustainable economic development" is identified as part of "A Vision for Action," in Vice President Gore's *Reinventing Environmental Management*,[141] environmental sustainability does not appear to be identified as a major goal of U.S. policy. The rhetoric is just not there. Yet environmental sustainability is a prerequisite to true economic sustainability because without it the life-support infrastructure will collapse. Economic sustainability can serve as an essential element of a future vision, but only if that vision encompasses environmental resources. In view of the world's growing population, shrinking material and energy resources, and increasingly stressed environment, efforts to cultivate a common vision of a sustainable future are warranted.

Partnerships for Pollution Prevention

Individual commitment is an essential element of success in partnerships for preventing pollution. By educating employees about the environmental aspects of their activities and requiring their participation in reducing or eliminating the associated environmental impacts, ISO 14001 fosters pollution prevention and encompasses elements of internal cultural change, including the establishment of trust, as well as builds an internal partnership for pollution prevention on the foundation of individual action.

> Clearly in the hierarchy, prevention is where we should be putting a lot of time and interest and money because with a focus on prevention, then you help put the responsibility on individuals, on companies, on industry and communities, and that's where it really belongs (EPA).

Since an individual working in an organization that values environmental protection is more likely to take actions and make decisions that are consistent with those values than he or she would be in an organization that does not, the individual, and consequently the organization, are likely to be considered more trustworthy by other stakeholders. "The whole shift should be towards partnership, and then eventually [to] have the responsibility for the 'how to do something' in the hands of the private-sector" (SG).

A Step-Wise Process

Movement toward environmental partnership between government and industry is likely to progress more as a multi-step process than as a clean leap of faith. Industry, as discussed earlier, already has forward motion in this regard. Significant steps must now be taken by government to allow this process to continue. "EPA ... has got to become more balanced between conducting enforcement, and providing assistance and pollution prevention and opportunities for innovation on the other hand" (EPA). Industry would thus be provided with additional opportunities to demonstrate its ability to act responsibly and would increasingly be entrusted to self-direct more and more of its environment-related activities.

The approach taken by one state is to encourage industry to move away from needing environmental discharge permits by modifying product designs, raw material selections, and production processes to eliminate regulated emissions. One sequence of events envisioned for industry is to: (1) move from end-of-pipe strategies to in-process strategies with the goal of zero emissions, thus eliminating the need for permits, (2) expand their area of concern and responsibility to extend beyond the boundaries of the organization to reduce or eliminate life-cycle environmental costs, and (3) move toward sustainability by asking, and answering, the questions:

> Is it sustainable for us to be tapping into the raw materials that we're using or are we stressing our raw material usage? Should we be beginning to think about take-back schemes so that we don't have to go to the energy costs, the extraction cost and all that sort of stuff for our raw material? Is what we're producing recallable and can we use it? Can we move into green design (SG)?

The questions posed in the preceding paragraph illuminate the juncture of environment and economy and present appropriate considerations regarding the use of non-renewable resources. As the world population increases, demand for goods and services will grow, intensifying competition for material, energy, and environmental resources. "The most enlightened companies now are saying, if we don't head toward sustainable development, if we don't start to look at our raw material usage and our stresses on the environment, we will not be in business. We can't as a world, maintain this" (SG). As the yet to be determined steady-state human carrying capacity of the planet is approached, the buffering capacities of our natural systems will diminish. While there will always be regional variation, it will become more likely that an environmental calamity like a major oil spill or chemical release will have noticeable global impacts.

Possible Futures

One projected future places government regulatory enforcement at the bottom of a preferred hierarchy of social control mechanisms. This would be a system ...

> ... first of all, that relied on the demonstrated environmental responsibility of the private sector, and where you had to have some kind of regulatory approach, that the first line of reliance would be on third party systems, and then, somewhere down the line would be actual criminal enforcement — but that would be highly unusual (EPA).

In this scenario, environmental crime would be treated similarly to other crimes, i.e., the citizen (corporate or otherwise) would be assumed innocent. Standard operating procedure for regulatory agencies would be non-intrusive.

In the sustainable society, business would incorporate environmental concerns at every step of planning and implementation. "The role of business is ... first of all to understand and anticipate changes in demand in a way that fully embraces ecological and environmental considerations" (NGO). An educated and involved public would be aware of both the environmental and the economic aspects of commerce and business and:

> ... recognize really what the true costs and the true benefits are ... and ... make sure that both the costs and the benefits are equitably shared... . which means ... that government has some obligation to share some of the costs, because they are sharing some of the benefits (IEM).

Appendix

Journal of Private-Sector Environmental Management: 1970–1990

1970

Environmental Laws

❑ National Environmental Policy Act of 1969 (NEPA), enacted in 1970, required environmental impact statements for all actions undertaken by federal agencies including:

  * identifying environmental impacts of proposed actions
  * identifying alternatives to the proposed actions
  * addressing the relationship between short-term and long-term use of environmental resources
  * integrating social science considerations into decision processes

  With regard to alleged violations of NEPA, this Act provided standing for anyone with a "trifle" of injury to bring suit in a federal court.

❑ Resource Recovery Act (Solid Waste Disposal Act Amendments) directed the emphasis of solid waste management programs from disposal to recycling, and the reuse of recoverable materials.

❑ Clean Air Act Amendments:

  * provided emission limits on stationary sources
  * identified hazardous air pollutants
  * established national emission standards for new motor vehicles
  * included provisions for citizen lawsuits
  * established National Ambient Air Quality Standards for particulates, CO, SO_4, Pb, NO_x, and O_3

❑ Occupational Safety and Health Act:

* established National Institute for Occupational Safety and Health (NIOSH) to conduct research and prepare comprehensive criteria to ensure adequate health and safety in the workplace
* instituted a facility inspection program

Events

- ❑ U.S. Environmental Protection Agency was created by President Nixon's Reorganizational Plan Number 3, combining 15 components of 5 separate departments, and housing for the first time responsibility for the protection of air, water, and land under one roof.
- ❑ Occupational Safety and Health Administration (OSHA) was created as the agency principally responsible for environmental health in the workplace, thereby dealing with a greater range of chemical exposures than EPA.

Citizen Actions

- ❑ Earth Day represented both the culmination of almost a decade of increasing concern about clean-up and control of pollution (spurred in 1962 by Rachel Carson's book, *Silent Spring*), and the conception of an environmental movement that would influence legislators and regulators to mandate management and enforcement programs that focused on environmental contamination.
- ❑ League of Conservation Voters

Environmental Management Outcomes

- ❑ The interconnectedness of air, water, and soil systems is increasingly becoming recognized by scientists.[142]
- ❑ Some environmental managers are optimistic about the benefits of having environmental governance consolidated in the new Environmental Protection Agency.[143]
- ❑ There is a call by some for a creation of a new discipline to manage environmental concerns.[144]
- ❑ Some feel that corporations should take on environmental responsibilities rather than wait for government agencies to dictate policies that are likely to be inefficient and expensive.[3] This sentiment is obviated by lack of available incentives and inequities among authoritative jurisdictions regarding environmental performance requirements;[14] corporations feel that any voluntary efforts would

only put them at an economic disadvantage, when competitors are not required to do the same.

- Many call for the establishment of national environmental standards to level the playing field.[145]
- Industries (principally chemical and petroleum) are beginning to devote significant R&D efforts toward developing effective pollution control technology, with a focus on sulfur oxides.[146]

1971

Environmental Laws

- Water Pollution Control Act Amendments

Events

- William Ruckelhaus announces new organization of EPA.[147]
- U.S. Department of Commerce encourages U.S. companies with capabilities in the pollution control field to exhibit at the international trade fair. U.S. firms already own more than 10 percent of the European market for imported pollution control products, but commerce is pointing out that increasing self-sufficiency in Europe poses a challenge to U.S. manufacturers.[148]
- EPA announces water pollution control is in the forefront of its concerns.
- EPA rejects Union Carbide's plan to reduce SO_2 emissions by 70 percent by September 1994. EPA calls for a April 1972 deadline.

Citizen Actions

- Founding of Greenpeace
- Founding of Sierra Club's Legal Defense Fund

Environmental Management Outcomes

- Interdisciplinary nature of environmental problem solving becoming increasingly recognized.[7]
- Federal actions now subject to NEPA, forcing environmental issues to be identified.

- The National Industrial Pollution Control Council (an organization of leaders of American Industry established in 1970 by President Nixon), reports that every major detergent manufacturer had undergone top-priority efforts to formulate a non-phosphate laundry detergent product.[149]
- Survey of 45 companies, representing 98 percent of U.S. crude oil refining capacity, indicates that the industry is spending more than $1.5 million per day for pollution control equipment and R&D.[150]
- Henry Ford II pledges that Ford Motor Company aims to minimize pollution from its manufacturing facilities and products. Ford spends $22.5 million on pollution control at a new casting center, and upgrades smoke and dust collection systems in a foundry in Cleveland; he expects to spend $45 million for pollution control in 1971.[151]
- "Today's technology is not adequate to supply the nation's growing electric needs without serious damage to the environment. Research and development efforts are not sufficient to produce answers as quickly as society needs them."[152]
- A trend toward the establishment of special pollution control groups in industrial companies continues. Out of 179 pollution-prone North American firms polled, 89 have set up such groups at the corporate level. The typical pollution-control executive has an engineering degree, and may exert considerable influence over major policy decisions in addition to his or her main job of implementing pollution control programs.[153]
- Dupont makes a three-year commitment to pollution control, and pledges $300 million over the next three years for air and water pollution control.[154]
- The Monsanto Corporation is developing an environmental public relations strategy. Three important elements of the strategy include keeping the public informed that the company is combating air and water pollution, selling the benefits of their products, and publicizing the development of pollution control technology pioneered by the company. They claim that in matters of environmental public relations, reputation is highly important and it is achieved by good performance and good communication.[155]
- "Industry has changed its attitude toward environmental concerns so radically and in so short a time that environmentalist distrust of the change is both apparent and understandable." "... industry's remarkable metamorphosis from inward-looking chrysalis to socially responsible butterfly is both real and encouraging. And it is a major fact that it surely is going to enable us to win the short-term war against pollution; the long-term war is another matter."[156]

❑ "Con Ed is calling for a revision of the lengthy, often overlapping and always cumbersome series of reviews of reviews and permits required by city, county, state and federal jurisdictions before any new project can be located, approved, constructed or operated. What is needed "is a way to bring environmental issues into focus at an early stage of planning and get the issues resolved quickly."[157]

1972

Environmental Laws

❑ Water Pollution Control Act's goals:
  * by 1983, to clean the nation's water to provide for protection and propagation of fish, shellfish, and wildlife, and to provide for recreation in and on the water
  * by 1985, to eliminate all pollutant discharges

❑ Consumer Product Safety Act provided a mechanism for consumers to evaluate product safety and to protect against hazardous products, and led to the development of the Consumer Product Safety Commission.

Events

❑ United Nations Conference on the Human Environment led to the creation of the UN Environmental Program (UNEP), and marked the beginning of a global effort to protect the environment.

❑ Limits to Growth, the Club of Rome's report on the "Predicament of Mankind" is published:
  * examines the problem of environmental deterioration among others including the arms race, the population explosion, and economic stagnation
  * predicts a collapse of our systems of survival if trends continue without major intervention

Citizen Actions

❑ *Laissez faire* is dead, and there is a heightened concern among consumers about the safety of the products they buy

Environmental Management Outcomes

- According to Orville Freemen, President of Business International Corp., industry is concerned that the European Economic Community will adopt stringent environmental protection standards.[158]
- Steel industry guarantees that all steel cans produced in the U.S. now contain at least 25 percent recycled material.
- Proctor and Gamble begins listing ingredients on all packages of household laundry, dishwashing, and cleaning products to ensure consumers of its continued commitment to providing information about its products.
- The Council on Economic Priorities says that the pulp and paper industry will have adequate pollution control in most of its mills by 1975.[159]
- Environmental manager described as someone who needs skills in or knowledge of: process control technology as it relates to pollution abatement, legislative processes at all levels of government, negotiation with regulatory agencies, and corporate planning and personnel administration.
- Survey of North American industries reveals organizational emphasis on pollution control, typically from the top corporation manager with access to the president, whose principal responsibility to reconcile the need for environmental protection with the need for the company to make money.
- A.J. von Frank, Director of Environmental Control for Allied Chemical, is quoted as describing environmental management as "... piecing together a solution from seemingly irreconcilable parts ... not a matter of slick political compromising ... has to be a more rational input, mostly technical and economic."
- Jerome Wilkenfeld, Director of Environmental Health for Hooker Chemical Company, describes his job as " ...largely one of coordinating corporate policy at the pre-crisis stage, consulting with control agencies to set forth the industry position, working for effective legislation and educating plant managers so they know what's required of them." His general charge is to do what's necessary to see that Hooker is in compliance with environmental regulations, reporting to a VP and frequently to the President when necessary. He provides legal and technical information to plant managers, and acts as an advocate for plant managers interested in getting funds for pollution control.[160]
- Spending for pollution control in 1971 totaled 1.6 percent of U.S. GNP.[161]

1973

Environmental Laws

- ❑ Endangered Species Act is created which prohibits activities that harm endangered species, and designates areas of critical habitat.
- ❑ New Jersey introduces a bill, modeled upon a pioneering law based in Michigan in 1970, that would enable citizens to file damage suits against polluters.[162]

Events

- ❑ Creation of the Consumer Product Safety Commission enabled the establishment of consumer rights, including:
  - * safety from hazards in voluntarily consumed products
  - * safety from involuntary hazardous exposures
  - * provision of product information
  - * protection from fraud
  - * accessibility to government regarding related issues
- ❑ Small is Beautiful, by E.F. Schumacher, is published.
- ❑ Creation of the Cousteau Society

Environmental Management Outcomes

- ❑ Union Carbide's SHARE (Safety Health and Affairs Related to the Environment) program is organized in March of 1973. It is responsible for communicating, protecting, and improving the environment for in-plant conditions for more than 80,000 employees. SHARE exists within the Chemicals and Plastic division, and its aim is to reduce to a minimum, or eliminate, all toxic pollutants. All new projects must be approved for environmental safety and health features by SHARE. About half of SHARE's expenses go toward water pollution projects, and the remaining half goes evenly toward air pollution and the managing solid wastes.[163]
- ❑ Leading New Jersey industrialists complain that if New Jersey passes a law providing citizens legal standing to sue polluters, industry and transportation will grind to a halt.[164]

1974

Environmental Laws

- ❑ Safe Drinking Water Act assures the protection of the nation's groundwaters.

Events

- ❑ In Flixborough, England, 45 tons of cyclohexene leaked from a facility, causing an explosion and killing 28 people.

Environmental Management Outcomes

- ❑ Pollution control costs totaled $27.2 billion in 1974, accounting for 1.9 percent of the GNP. According to the Department of Commerce's Bureau of Economic Analysis:
  - * 94 percent of anti-pollution spending was for products and services to reduce pollutant emission
  - * 6 percent was for regulation, monitoring, research, and development
  - * from 1972 to 1974, the component devoted to atmospheric emissions rose 66 percent[165]

1975

Environmental Laws

- ❑ Congress' Joint Economic Committee concludes that the economic impacts associated with compliance to the nation's environmental regulations is likely to produce more jobs than are lost, and that the effect on the prices of goods should be negligible.[166]
- ❑ EPA is determined to give unified and coordinated direction to the pollution control effort without complex regulations.[167]

Events

- ❑ Love Canal is publicized, and the world became informed of the high incidences of chemically induced illness, exposure to burning and nausea producing chemical fumes, and chemical seepage into residential basements occurring at Love Canal.

Citizen Actions

❑ Environmental activists have moved into *the system*:

* Dennis Hayes, National Coordinator of Earth Day 1970, is Energy Coordinator for the State of Illinois
* Glenn Paulson, Earth Day Steering Committee member, is Assistant Commissioner at NJDEP
* Claire Dedrick and Larry Moss, both former Sierra Club leaders, are Secretary and Deputy Secretary for the State of California's Office of Natural Resources[168]

Environmental Management Outcomes

❑ Major chemical companies acknowledge gains made by environmentalists, while both learn how to play the game: [169]

* DuPont claims that Earth Day 1975 drew little attention "... because dramatic environmental progress has been made and because much of the 1970 rhetoric is now the law of the land."
* Dow Chemical says that environmental activists are more effective now than five years ago, "And they've left the streets and gone to court," adds an environmental manager from another chemical company. However, an Environmental Manager at Monsanto says "Environmental control is achieved by engineering, not litigation," and the director of Ohio's EPA adds that "Once you get into court, the polluter is off the hook until the court case is settled." Chicago's Lake Michigan Federation, an environmentalist group, claims that some industries use the grace period afforded them by lengthy legal battles to maximize use of the operations being questioned.
* There is a general consensus among the chemical industry that upper management is more perceptive regarding the need to finance pollution control. Every new development has an environmental budget.
* DuPont authorizes 13 percent of its planned capital expenditures for pollution control.
* Union Carbide claims that within one year it will have more employees working in the environment than in sales.

❑ There is concern among some in industry that the call for increased social responsibility and greater public accountability could ultimately drive us away from free enterprise and toward a socialist democracy in which government has access to confidential decision-making, and could force disclosure of information for use in environmental enforcement actions.[170]

- ❑ Increasingly, financial managers in business are becoming involved in development of measurements for social responsibility and communication of environmentally related financial statement information.[171]

1976

Environmental Laws

- ❑ Toxic Substance Control Act (TSCA):
  - * created to fill gaps between existing regulations governing the use of hazardous materials in commerce
  - * requires manufacturers to develop substantial data about new chemicals and submit it to EPA for review before producing and distributing it
  - * provides EPA with the authority to require manufacturers to conduct extensive testing if EPA determines there is an unreasonable risk of exposure to the chemical and/or insufficient data to make a reasonable assessment
  - * requires manufacturers to keep records of any significant adverse health effects associated with its products
  - * provides EPA with authority to prohibit the manufacturing of a chemical
- ❑ Safe Drinking Water Act Amendments
- ❑ Resource Conservation and Recovery Act:
  - * presented guidelines for solid waste management
  - * provided a legal basis for implementation of those guidelines and standards for solid waste treatment, storage, and disposal
  - * addressed both hazardous waste and solid waste, with preferential timelines given to the hazardous wastes
  - * emphasized hazardous wastes through the mid 80s, then shifted to municipal solid waste
  - * established cradle-to-grave coverage
  - * established waste tracking systems
- ❑ Tax Reform Act of 1976 provides a 60-month amortization period for pollution control facilities. Under this law, 50 percent of the investment becomes available as a tax credit.[172]

Environmental Management Outcomes

- ❑ Environmental Management is classified as a discipline, but the definition is still fluid. Characteristics of Environmental Management include:
  - * systematic rather than linear
  - * deals with interplay between economic and environmental imperatives
  - * deals with interplay between short-term and long-term issues
  - * transdisciplinary
  - * an advocacy discipline
  - * probablistic — dealing with uncertainties of the future
  - * involved with ethics[173]
- ❑ Spending for pollution control in the U.S. totaled 1.8 percent of the nation's GNP.[174]

1977

Environmental Laws

- ❑ Clean Water Act:
  - * defined and established national effluent limitations for toxic pollutants, conventional pollutants non-conventional, and non-toxic pollutants (e.g., ammonia & chlorine)
  - * established national water quality standards
  - * established National Pollutant Discharge Elimination System permit program
  - * authorized increased penalties for violations
- ❑ Clean Air Act Amendments:
  - * provided for prevention of significant deterioration
  - * established non-attainment areas
  - * provided for emission offsets

Environmental Management Outcomes

- ❑ The Environmental Industry Council, an organization of representatives of pollution control equipment manufacturers and trade associations, is formed. Its purpose is to provide information, provide a referral service, and give national awards for effective pollution abatement programs.[175]

- The environmental management issue is identified as the need to create incentives (either positive or negative) in order to induce action.
  - * Its targets are to reduce residuals generation, modify residuals after generation, make better use of the assimilative capacity of the environment, and increase the assimilative capacity of the environment.
  - * Its incentives include the regulatory, the economic, the administrative, the judicial, and the educational.
  - * No single management strategy will be best for all situations.[176]
- Industry supports the concept of an *emission bank*, providing a system of appropriate economic incentives to move toward environmental goals. This would require industry to competitively bid for pollution permits for its pollution sources. The number of permits would be limited corresponding to a maximum pollutant loading set for a given region.[177]
- Industries in the U.S. are competitively disadvantaged in the world market by the high cost of mandated pollution control.[178]
  - * There is a call for the President to enforce existing laws that require promotion of international environmental standards through treaties.
  - * Pollution standards vary around the world but are usually less stringent than those in the U.S.
  - * Litigation as a means of environmental protection is used more frequently in the U.S. than in other countries.

1978

Environmental Laws

- RCRA Amendments
- EPA allows companies discretion in reducing pollution by establishing the "bubble" concept of an industrial site. The company can reduce or increase its emissions from any particular source within the "bubble," as long as the net result is an overall reduction. This will allow industry to focus its efforts on areas in which there is more opportunity for innovation.[179]
- There will be an increased emphasis in 1978 on the control of toxic substances, especially those suspected of being carcinogens.[180]

Events

- ❑ Love Canal is evacuated, approximately 800 houses were bought, and almost 1,000 families were relocated through government programs. This evacuation was pivotal in the passage of the Comprehensive Environmental Response, Compensation and Liability Act of 1980.
- ❑ In Seveso, Italy, two kilograms of dioxin escaped from a plant, killing thousands of animals and causing the evacuation of 70,000 people which lasted for many years.
- ❑ Air pollution emission rights are now entering the market, rights are limited by EPA.[181]

Environmental Management Outcomes

- ❑ The American Chemical Society's recommendations on control of environmental pollution include:[182]
  - * continue to make improvements in analytical chemical methods to monitor the environment
  - * develop better statistical methods for relating monitoring requirements to the desired data
  - * gather more reliable data to define normal and deviant trends in concentration levels of contaminants in the environment
  - * develop a better understanding of how contaminants affect natural systems, especially with regard to long-term, low-level exposure
  - * develop better municipal wastewater treatment technology
  - * pay more attention to decontamination of equipment contaminated with radioactivity
- ❑ The control of air pollution is still the largest environmental cost in the chemical industry. Overall environmental spending is expected to decrease in 1978 to $661 million from $717 million in 1977, and $821 million in 1976. However, new regulations under the Water Pollution Control Act, governing hazardous waste discharges to water bodies and under RCRA governing disposal, is expected to drive spending back up to 1976 levels.[183]
- ❑ There is a need to view business as a social institution.[184] Though historically society establishes values and norms for business to follow, the complexity of environmental problems puts business in a unique position of responding to pressure from consumers, environmental groups, international affiliates, etc.:

* business is increasingly recognizing pollution as an international concern
* companies have come to regard environmental costs, even involuntary costs, as a normal part of doing business
* a majority of chief executives favor stronger pollution legislation

1979

Events

- Three Mile Island release
- J. E. Lovelock's "Gaia Hypothesis"[185]

Environmental Management Outcomes

- An environmental manager at Mobil Chemical predicts that by 1986, every American family will pay at least $2,500 for the enforcement of environmental law without receiving any improvement in health as a result.[186]

1980

Environmental Laws

- RCRA Amendments
- Comprehensive, Environmental Response, Compensation and Liability Act (CERCLA), otherwise know as Superfund, was enacted to respond to problems at uncontrolled hazardous waste sites. Its functions include:
  * granting EPA authority to enforce or conduct clean-ups where it determines there is an imminent and substantial danger to health or the environment
  * providing EPA with the means to recover its clean-up costs from responsible parties

  * establishing joint and several liability for contributors to hazardous waste sites

Events

- ❑ Lawsuits were filed against Allied Chemical Company for damages resulting from the mismanagement of Kepone, a suspect carcinogen, by one of its subcontractors, Life Science Products. Allied has since stopped Kepone production.

Citizen Actions

- ❑ Consumption behavior analyses are revealing that environmentally responsible target markets are becoming increasingly significant and may warrant development of environment-oriented consumer affairs or marketing programs.[187]

Environmental Management Outcomes

- ❑ Allied Chemical Company has incorporated environmental responsibility into its new incentive-compensation plan, and has developed and implemented new procedures for monitoring the environmental decision-making of plant personnel.[188]
- ❑ Environmental Managers from 39 chemical companies predict hazardous waste disposal will be their biggest environmental problem in the future.[189]
  * One environmental manager said, "There's got to be a place for waste — you can't make it disappear. If you take it out of the air, you've got to put it in the water or the land. You take it out of the water, you've got to put in the air or the land. You take it out of the land, you've got to put in the air or water. It's Catch-22."
  * Most considered the costs of complying with environmental regulations to be excessive and inflationary.
  * Most companies used landfills for waste disposal.
  * There was general agreement that TSCA will stifle new-product development and as a result companies will tend to develop only larger-volume or very high-return products.
  * Another environmental manager said that the chemical industry's image problem is exacerbating the difficulties they are having in the environmental arena.

1981

Events

- Interior Secretary James Watt proposes (unsuccessfully) eliminating the provision of the Clean Air Act which required new power plants to reduce sulfur emissions, and instead recommends (unsuccessfully) that states set their own ambient pollution standards.[190]

Environmental Management Outcomes

- Two Owens-Illinois employees from its plastic bottle cap plant in Brookville, Pennsylvania, are apprehended dumping waste solvents into an abandoned strip mine. Several years earlier, Olin chemical found employees falsifying environmental records at its Niagara Falls, New York chlorine plant. These events are considered by the industry to be incredible at companies of this size.[191] Environmental managers can't be aware of every decision made by a company's employees, so they must put management-assurance systems in place. Surveillance and control are necessary.
- Petroleum industry representatives are supporting a House Bill provision that will allow federal oil spill liability legislation to preempt that of the states. The concern was to move away from a fragmented approach that would tie up large amounts of industry money in clean-up funds, and increase costs to consumers.[192]

1982

Environmental Laws

- EPA proposes to reform regulations to include the "bubble" policy of considering all source of pollution at an individual plant as a single source, establish an offset policy allowing states to increase pollution at one site by reducing elsewhere, and establish banking policy granting pollution credits for current reductions to be used for future increases. Congress rejects these proposals, but *de facto* deregulation is accomplished by budget and personnel cuts, reducing enforcement and development of standards.[193]
- Rita M. Lavelle's nomination as EPA administrator for solid waste and emergency response is opposed by environmental groups because of her association with Aerojet-General Corporation, a firm

claimed to have one of the worst dump sites in the U.S. Lavelle says that she prefers to use the *carrot* rather than the *stick* when dealing with industry.[194]

- ❑ EPA is criticized by Senator John Chafee for incomplete hazardous waste regulations six years after RCRA's enactment and for the slow movement of Superfund money to the states two years after CERCLA' s enactment.[195]
- ❑ EPA Administrator Anne Gorsuch and Interior Secretary James Watt are known for their industry ties, and the Reagan Administration draws criticism for policies that are harming the environment.[196]
- ❑ The absence of "*body count*" on the dockets of the Justice department is identified as evidence of EPA's lack of enforcement efforts.[197]
- ❑ EPA establishes regulations governing land disposal of wastes and estimates the cost to industry will be at least $1 billion per year. The Environmental Defense Fund had sued EPA to force it to issue these long-deferred rules.[198]

Events

- ❑ A special 1982 issue of the UNEP publication *Industry and Environment: The Next Decade* focuses on waste reduction.[199]

Environmental Management Outcomes

- ❑ In response to confusion brought about by the conflict between EPA's mission and the Reagan Administration's lack of support for the Agency and federal aid for the states, industry has adopted a wait-and-see attitude regarding environmental compliance.[200]
- ❑ Otto Koch, Executive Director of Bayer in West Germany, claims that the declared aim in an age of cleaner technology is to:
  - * minimize waste by developing new products that will be less of a burden to man and the environment during use and handling, and by developing new ways to make existing products using techniques that cause inherently less waste in the course of manufacture
  - * utilize waste by recycling
  - * degrade that part of the remainder which can neither be reduced in mass ... nor reused
  - * dispose of only that part which is non-degradable and consists of ... inorganic byproducts[201]

1983

Events

- Rita M. Lavelle is fired as EPA administrator for solid waste and emergency response for her refusal to use enforcement mechanisms on businesses to clean up toxic waste dumps.[202]
- A Labor Department administrative law judge decides in favor of Hugh Kaufman and against EPA under the *whistleblower protection provisions of* CERCLA. Kaufman had been harassed by the Agency for testifying in front of Congress.[203]
- EPA Administrator Anne M. Burford resigns over allegations of political manipulation, mismanagement, and conflicts of interest.[204]
- William Ruckelshaus is nominated for EPA Administrator.[205]

Environmental Management Outcomes

- In spite of the cradle-to-grave requirements of RCRA, 80 percent of hazardous wastes are still going to landfills, but a growing number of chemical companies are incinerating their wastes. This move toward incineration is driven by proposed RCRA amendments that would severely restrict land disposal of such wastes, and by the potential for reducing or eliminating the long-term liability associated with land burial of hazardous wastes.[206]

1984

Environmental Laws

- RCRA Amendments
- Hazardous & Solid Waste Amendments
- OSHA Amendments:
    * Hazard Communication Standard (29 CFR 1910.1200) — "Worker Right-to-Know," requires employers to identify hazardous materials in the workplace and inform employees of the hazards utilizing labeling, material Safety Data Sheets (MSDS), and training to do so.

Events

- ❑ U.S. Securities and Exchange Commission now requires certain firms to make pollution disclosure reports available for potential investors.[207]
- ❑ Sustainable development defined is as: "... future generations remain at least as well off as current generations."[208]
- ❑ Bhopal, India: over 3,000 killed and 200,000 injured when a Union Carbide plant leaks approximately 45 tons of methyl isocyanate.

1985

Events

- ❑ British scientists report a hole in the ozone layer over Antarctica in the Spring.[209]
- ❑ Sustainable development defined as: "Current decisions should not impair the prospects for maintaining or improving future living standards."[210]

Environmental Management Outcomes

- ❑ The cost of protecting the environment is identified as having the following elements:
    - * diversion of capital from productive investments to pollution control investments (which are non-productive)
    - * depletion of scarce economic and human resources for the design, operation, and maintenance of pollution control equipment
    - * additional cost and delays associated with the introduction of new products
    - * disruption of plans for developing new production facilities and markets
- ❑ (Some believe that the greatest cost to industry has been in the development of a negative image of technology.)[211]
- ❑ Virtually all major companies now have environmental policies, and virtually all of them internally allocate environmental responsibilities.[212]
- ❑ There is evidence that industrial attitudes have changed over the last decade (1975–1985):

  * The major emphasis has been on abating pollution but industry has advanced its thinking about other environmental issues such as conservation of resources and recycling.
  * An emphasis on prevention rather than cure is being echoed by industry leaders around the world.[213]

- ❑ The Bhopal tragedy shifted the emphasis of industry from remedial, technically-based environmental programs to preventative, socially-based programs, and from an attitude of throwing money at a problem to one of education and the development of cleaner projects, processes, and products.[214]
- ❑ World-wide awareness is growing that pollution prevention can be justified economically. The slogan "Pollution Prevention Pays" does not come from an academic institute, but from the 3M Company.[215]

1986

Environmental Laws

- ❑ Superfund Amendments and Reauthorization Act includes three Titles, all of which carry out different functions.
  * Title I provided an additional $8.4 billion to carry on the work of CERCLA.
  * Title II establishes goals for completing remedial activities, provides worker right-to-know requirements at hazardous waste sites and at spills of hazardous materials, and establishes the Hazardous Waste Operations and Emergency Response (HazWOper) training requirement for employees working in areas where exposure is possible.
  * Title III is known as the Emergency Preparedness and Community Right-to-Know Act
    - ⇒ establishes emergency planning committees that must include industry officials
    - ⇒ requires emergency notification in the case of releases
    - ⇒ requires preparation and availability of Material Safety Data Sheets at facilities covered by the Act
    - ⇒ requires facilities to submit detailed information regarding the exact location and quantities of hazardous materials or waste being stored on the site

⇒ provides for information collected under this program to be available to the public, with certain exceptions for trade secrets

⇒ provides for civil and criminal penalties

Events

❑ The Chernobyl nuclear plant explodes.[216]

Environmental Management Outcomes

❑ Waste management firms that treat and incinerate hazardous wastes are appearing in the marketplace as an alternative to those that bury such wastes. The attraction is the reduced potential for future liability of the generators.[217]

1987

Environmental Laws

❑ Clean Water Act Amendments

❑ New federal regulations require employees who work with hazardous wastes to complete 40 hours of safety training. This training activity is specified in OSHA Interim Final Rule (29 CFR 1910.120).[218]

Events

❑ ISO 9000

❑ Socially responsible investment has become a means of expressing philosophical protest.[219]

  * Estimates indicate that nearly $200 billion worth of investment is currently being screened and the trend is increasing.

  * Environmental responsibility is included among the major social responsibilities identified by investors.

❑ Delegates of 24 nations develop and sign a pact called the Montreal Protocol to reduce CFCs. This is the first such global agreement to protect the environment. Involved were scientists, environmentalists, and industrial representatives. The Protocol allowed developing countries to increase CFC use over the next ten years.[220]

- "Brundtland Report": "Sustainable development is development that meets the needs of the present without compromising the ability of future generations to meet their own needs."[221]

1988

Environmental Laws

- New Jersey, Connecticut, and Massachusetts have each enacted an *Environmental Clean-Up and Responsibility Act* (ECRA) to address the issue of potential Superfund liability associated with property transfers.[222]

Events

- President George Bush identifies environmental issues as hallmarks of his administration and promises:
  - greater use of economic and market incentives to reach environmental goals
  - more attention to prevention of pollution then to end-of-pipe clean-ups
  - more emphasis on individual exposure to pollutants then on ambient concentrations
  - better support for long term research and development programs[223]
- Project 88, initiated by Senators Timothy Wirth and John Heinz, puts together a 50-member team from academia, industry, the environmental community, and government to evaluate the use of market forces to protect the environment. Project 88's functions include:
  - addressing the new environmentalism which embraces market orientation as a legitimate approach to environmental protection
  - identifying the Environmental Defense Fund as the first of the major environmental organizations to advocate incentive based policies
  - identifying some previous uses of economic incentives for environmental protection including EPA's emission trading program, tradable permits for water pollution control, innovative water transfers, and bottle bills[224]

  * The article discusses the use of market forces to supplement the regulatory power of the government and to create a setting for private sector innovation and initiative.

Environmental Management Outcomes

- ❑ Mergers and acquisition of industrial properties have been slowed in the face of potential Superfund liability:
  * In order to reduce exposure to such liability, many companies are leasing rather than buying properties.
  * Purchasing companies are demanding that the sellers indemnify them against all related actions.
  * There is a call for government to set a policy to protect potential buyers.[225]
- ❑ Sandoz Chemical Corporation develops a way to eliminate the use of potentially hazardous solvents in the production of its vat dyes. Sandoz hopes to capitalize on this environmental breakthrough to recoup its R&D investment and increase its market share.[226]

1989

Environmental Laws

- ❑ Protection of natural resources by empowering courts to order a company to provide financial relief for environmental restoration is clearly established in federal environmental law.[227]
  * Congress is expanding the doctrine's applicability regarding: who can sue and how much can be requested.
  * Congress embraces the concept of allowing citizens to sue to enforce environmental law.

Events

- ❑ The Exxon Valdez oil spill occurs in Prince William Sound.
- ❑ Social responsibility is determined to provide a potentially rewarding selection criterion for investors.[228]
  * Surveys showed that investments in socially sensitive stocks over the five-year period from 1984 through 1988 returned 31 percent more than Standard & Poor.

* Selection criteria for social responsibility included limited business (less than 4 percent) in weapons, alcohol, tobacco, gambling, and nuclear power, environmental responsibility, compliance with worker safety regulations, and fair treatment of employees.
* There is a developing trend among investment companies toward socially responsible funds.

Environmental Management Outcomes

- ❑ The electronics industry criticizes itself for only grudgingly agreeing to meet current standards and for shortsightedness regarding planning to meet future legislation.
  * Concerns for the industry revolve around:[229]
    - ⇒ the quality of atmospheric emissions from smokestacks
    - ⇒ the quality of water discharged to sewers
    - ⇒ the health and safety of its employees
  * Driving the industry's concerns are:
    - ⇒ new upcoming environmental legislation that is supported by the Bush administration
    - ⇒ public pressure boosted by the Exxon Valdez oil spill
    - ⇒ the Montreal Protocol mandating elimination of CFC production by the year 2000
    - ⇒ recent court decisions that held companies, rather than their insurance companies, responsible for hazardous waste clean-ups
  * A blueprint for environmental action in the electronics industry is recommended:
    - ⇒ set up an environmental action team of senior executives
    - ⇒ launch an aggressive campaign to minimize hazardous waste with use-reduction targets and a use-elimination preference
    - ⇒ establish a waste reduction and safety philosophy among the workers
    - ⇒ integrate worker health and safety into the environmental safety mission
    - ⇒ open up a dialogue with local environmental regulators and environmental groups
    - ⇒ push accountability for hazardous waste generation to the lowest level

⇒ work with suppliers to minimize hazardous material use and develop safe handling practices

⇒ share data on use-reduction practices with others in industry, including competitors

⇒ extend waste treatment services at cost or for a nominal fee to small firms within region

⇒ work with legislators to develop appropriate environmental initiatives at local, state and federal levels

⇒ explore new waste reduction equipment and services

⇒ inform local communities and media of hazardous materials in use before required to do so

⇒ initiate R&D of less hazardous chemical substitutes and processes

1990

Environmental Laws

❏ Pollution Prevention Act

❏ Oil Pollution Act

❏ Clean Air Act Amendments

- focus on acid deposition
- focus on ozone layer depletion
- stronger non-attainment focus
- federal permit system
- increased civil and criminal penalties

Events

❏ A study performed by Deloitte & Touche and the Stanford University Graduate School of Business reveals that American businesses are acknowledging the relationship between their future success in the marketplace and public perception regarding their environmental performance. The study revealed:[230]

- Regulatory issues continue to dominate environmental concerns and activities in business.
- Associated costs have evolved during the period of 1973 to 1990, from an "*excessive annoyance*" to a normal business cost.

  ⇒ Seventy-five percent of the companies surveyed had paid penalties for violations of environmental regulations.
  ⇒ Average fines were as high as $300,000.
* Two-thirds of companies expected more stringent environmental regulations in the future.
* Well over 90 percent of the responders held environmental issues as important strategic considerations.
* "Companies are transitioning [away from regulatory compliance as the principal motivator] to proactive environmental policies" The transition was thought to be in its infancy but being driven quickly into the heart of financial and strategic plans by consumer and regulatory pressures.
* 31 percent of the responders had policies on recycling
* 26 percent of the responders had policies on energy conservation
* 25 percent of the responders had policies on environmental image issues
* 20 percent of the responders were involved in green labeling
* Companies face four critical challenges in the management of their environmental strategy:
  ⇒ regulatory compliance
  ⇒ environmental risk management
  ⇒ marketing response
  ⇒ integration of environmental strategies
* Consumer and competitive market forces are moving environmental issues to the heart of American business strategy.

Citizen Actions

❑ The Coalition for Environmentally Responsible Economies (CERES) has been working to persuade thousands of U.S. companies to develop responsible corporate environmental policies based upon ten principles symbolically called the "Valdez Principles."[231]
  * There is a considerable amount of resistance due to the requirement that participants must develop and make available, a comprehensive annual environmental assessment report card.

Environmental Management Outcomes

❑ A global community of concern for the environment is beginning to develop.[232]

- ❑ In industry, this concern is being manifested by developing, publicizing, and adhering to environmental visions, missions, and codes of ethics.[233]
- ❑ Industry is trying to conduct business without damaging the environment in order to restore its credibility with the public.[234]
- ❑ Companies are beginning to discover that good environmental performance can yield dividends in avoided costs and in recognition as environmentally responsible corporate citizens.[235]
  - * Manufacturers are increasingly involved in joint recycling ventures, waste minimization, substitution of toxic chemicals, waste treatment, and reduction of the use of chlorofluorocarbons.
- ❑ Driven by the increasing availability and accessibility to the public of industry-specific environmental information, pressure on industry to become more environmentally responsible is predicted for the next decade.[236]
- ❑ Public power utilities now include environmental responsibility as a building block for, and a requisite part of, the development process for every policy they create.[237]
- ❑ DuPont Canada has developed an environmental policy and established its own set of environmental principles and goals[238] which include:
  - * waste reduction in its manufacturing processes
  - * reusing waste materials from existing operations
  - * recycling waste plastics and other waste materials
  - * DuPont is investing in research to increase production efficiency and to make products more environmentally benign.
    - ⇒ Environmental communication strategies are being developed or enhanced in order to help consumers make informed choices and to get the word out about what is being accomplished at DuPont.
- ❑ The chemical industry has established the "*Responsible Care*" program in response to pressures to develop responsible corporate environmental policies. There is concern among critics that this program represents more of a public relations effort than it does a move toward real progress.[239]

References

1. **Hawkins, George S.,** Senior Advisor to the Office of Assistance and Pollution Prevention, U.S. Environmental Protection Agency, Region I, Telephone interview by author, Boston, MA, August 5, 1996.
2. **USEPA,** *Partnerships in Preventing Pollution. 100-B-96-001,* Spring 1996.
3. **Hawkins, George S.,** Senior Advisor to the Office of Assistance and Pollution Prevention, U.S. Environmental Protection Agency, Region I. Interview by author, Boston, MA, August 5, 1996.
4. **Cushman, John,** Feds plan probe of pollution standards: Pa. Among states that may shirk EPA laws. *The New York Times,* December 15, 1996.
5. Enforcement: EPA says some states are too lax on pollution, *Greenwire,* December 16, 1996.
6. **USEPA,** The Common Sense Initiative: A New Generation of Environmental Protection.
7. **USEPA,** *Partnerships in Preventing Pollution, 100-B-96-001,* Spring 1996.
8. Project XL: Minnesota's Enviro. Agency Suspends Program, *Greenwire,* August 29, 1996.
9. Minnesota, Charging EPA Input Inflexibility, Suspends its Pilot Project XL Efforts, *Environment Week,* 34(35), 1996.
10. Oversight: 3M, MPCA Protest EPA's Inflexibility of Companies Project XL Permit, *Hazardous Waste News,* 18(36), 1996.
11. Inflexibility? EPA Clings to Command and Control; 3M Shelves Project XL Proposal, *Environmental Remediation Technology,* 4(19), 1996.
12. 3M Quits Project XL, *Chemical Week,* 49, September 26, 1996.
13. **Fairley, Peter,** Frustrations with Project XL Mount, *Chemical Week,* 14, 1996.
14. Project XL: EPA Officials Move to Save Troubled Program, *Greenwire,* December 4, 1996.
15. EU States Approve ISO 14001 as Sole European Standard, *International Environmental Systems Update,* 3(9), 8, 19XX.
16. Japanese Trade Ministry Asks Firms to Prepare for ISO 14000, *International Environmental Systems Update,* 3(1), 1, 19XX.
17. **Fraust, C. L.,** Senior Staff Engineer, Lucent Technologies, Interview by author, Allentown, PA, August 1, 1996.
18. States Move to Coordinate ISO 14000 Pilot Project, *State Environmental Monitor,* 1(8), 13, 1996.
19. **Herman, Steven Al,** Assistant Administrator, USEPA, Office of Enforcement and Compliance Assurance, Internal memorandum to EPA Directors, June 25, 1996.
20. **McKiel, Mary,** Director, EPA Voluntary Standards Network, EPA Coordinator to the ISO 14000, Vice Chair U.S. TAG to TC-207, Interview by author, Washington, D.C., July 29, 1996.

21. States, Charging USEPA Bungled Project XL, Set Up Reform Group, *State Environmental Monitor,* 1(8), 3, 1996.
22. **Middleton, John T.,** A Fresh Opportunity for Industry, *ES&T,* 1(3), ACS, 1967.
23. **Middleton, John T.,** A Fresh Opportunity for Industry, *ES&T,* 1(3), ACS, 1967.
24. **Middleton, John T.,** A Fresh Opportunity for Industry, *ES&T,* 1(3), ACS, 1967.
25. **Sarnof, David,** Lake Erie, Dying but not Dead, *ES&T,* 1(3), ACS, 1967.
26. **Middleton, John,** Sulfur Oxides Must Be Controlled, *ES&T* 4(2), ACS, 1970.
27. **Hayes, Denis,** Earth Day was Just a Beginning, *ES&T,* 4(6), ACS, 1970.
28. **Doan, Herbert D.,** Viewpoint, *ES&T,* 4(3), ACS, 1970.
29. **Speer, Edgar B.,** Punitive Legislation is Not Needed, *ES&T,* 4(10), ACS, 1970.
30. **Bown, Michael,** Environmental Agency Makes Sense, *ES&T* 4(7), ACS, 1970.
31. **Zim, Marvin, H.,** Allied Chemical's $20-Million Ordeal, *Fortune* 98(5), 82, 1978.
32. **Tucker, Lewis R., Jr.,** Profiling Environmentally Responsible Consumer-Citizens, *Journal of the Academy of Marketing Science,* 9(4), 454, 1981.
33. Environmental Managers Face Some Solid Problems, *Chemical Week,* 122(20), 27, 1981.
34. **Luzzatto, Donald,** Social Investing: The Protest for the 1980's, *National Underwriter,* 91(4), 4, 1987.
35. **Smith, Andy,** Survey Claims Socially Selected Investments Can Provide Profitable Return, *Corporate Cashflow,* 10(4), 22, 1989.
36. **Rainey, John S.,** Innovative Energy, *Business & Economic Review,* 37(1), 39, 1990.
37. **Newall, J.E.,** Managing Environmental Responsibility, *Business Quarterly,* 55(2), 90, 1990.
38. **Barnard, Jayne, W.,** Exxon Collides with the 'Valdez Principles,' *Business & Society Review,* (74), 32, 1990.
39. Environmental Issue Management Moving to Heart of American Business Policies; New study profiles insight on corporate attitudes, *Financial News,* October 30, 1990.
40. **Sobel, Steven B.,** Challenge of the '90s', *Canadian Insurance,* 95(6), 22, 1990.
41. **Bostian, David B., Jr.,** Paradigms for Prosperity: Economic and Political Trends for the 1990 and Early 21st Century, *Futurist,* 24(4), 33, 1990.
42. **Silas, C.J.,** The Environment: Playing to Win, *Public Relations Journal,* 46(1), 10, 1990.
43. **Patterson, Timothy D.,** Preserving the Planet: A Mounting Problem, *World,* 24(1), 8, 1990.
44. **Rotman, David,** Environmental Regulation: How Mounting Public Pressures and New Legislation Will Reshape the Way Industry Does Business, *Chemical Week,* 145(13), 66, 1989.
45. **Taylor, Frederick W.,** *Scientific Management, Part II, The Principles of Scientific Management,* Harper & Row, New York, 1947.
46. **Fayol, Henri,** *General and Industrial Management,* Pitman Publishing, New York, 1949.
47. **McGregor, Douglas,** *The Human Side of Enterprise,* McGraw-Hill, New York, 1960.
48. **Dejon, William L.,** *Principles of Management: Text & Cases,* Benjamin/Cummings, Philippines, 1978, 184.
49. **Kazmier, Leonard J.,** *Principles of Management: A Program for Self-instruction,* McGraw-Hill, New York, 1969, 9.
50. **Kazmier, Leonard J.,** *Principles of Management: A Program for Self-instruction,* McGraw-Hill, New York, 1969, 15.

51. **Hitt, William D.,** *Management In Action: Guidelines for New Managers,* Battelle Press, XXX, 1985, 13.
52. **Morelli, John,** Survey of EHS professionals, Rochester Institute of Technology, November–February, 1997.
53. **West, Gordon A. and Michaud, Ronald W.,** *Principles of Environmental, Health & Safety Management,* Government Institutes, 1995, 12.
54. Total Quality Environmental Management, Global Environmental Management Initiative, 1992, 1.
55. **Deming, W. Edwards,** *Out of the Crisis,* W. Edwards Deming Institute, 1986, chap. 2.
56. **Wadhams, Jennifer L.,** EHS Management, lecture notes, Rochester Institute of Technology, Fall 1997.
57. **USEPA,** Project XL Facility Page, URL address: http://199.223.29.233/ProjectXL/xl_home.nsf/all/imb.html#legal, April 1, 1997.
58. **USEPA,** Information on the Various XL Projects, URL address: http://199.223.29.233/ProjectXL/xl_home.nsf/all/xl_info, April 1, 1997.
59. **Doan, Herbert D.,** Viewpoint, *ES&T,* 4(3), ACS, 1970.
60. **Yandle, Bruce,** Environmental Policy: Thoughts on a Positive Agenda, *Vital Speeches,* 62(16), 510, 1996.
61. **Hawkins, George S.,** Senior Advisor to the Office of Assistance and Pollution Prevention, U.S. Environmental Protection Agency, Region I, Telephone interview by author, Boston, MA, July 1996.
62. **Hawkins, George S.,** Senior Advisor to the Office of Assistance and Pollution Prevention, U.S. Environmental Protection Agency, Region 1, The Eagle Agenda: An Agenda for the Future of Environmental Protection.
63. **Haynsworth, Marion,** Integrating Regulatory Processes Applauded, *South Carolina Environmental Compliance Update,* 4(9), 1996.
64. The Alternative Path, *Chemical Week,* 44, October 9, 1996.
65. Remarks by Governor Tom Ridge, Three Rivers Environmental Awards, Pennsylvania Enforcement Council, Pittsburgh, Pennsylvania, May 28, 1996.
66. **USEPA,** The Common Sense Initiative: A New Generation of Environmental Protection, 1994.
67. **USEPA,** *Statement of Regulatory Priorities,* 60 CFR59658, November 20, 1995.
68. USEPA to Offer States New Role in Setting Enforcement Goals, *State Environmental Monitor,* 1(8), 10, 1996.
69. **Hansen, Fred,** Deputy Administrator, USEPA, Reinvention at EPA, Testimony before Senate Appropriation Committee, February 29, 1996.
70. **Phillips, Earl W., Jr., and Freeman, Brian,** Privatizing Environmental Regulation: From Do-As-You're Told to Do-It-Yourself, *Connecticut Law Tribune,* November 13, 1995.
71. **Yandle, Bruce,** Environmental Policy: Thoughts on a Positive Agenda, *Vital Speeches,* 62(16), 510, 1996.
72. *ISO 14000 Questions & Answers,* 3rd ed., CEEM, 1997.
73. EU States Approve ISO 14001 as Sole European Standard, *International Environmental Systems Update,* 3(9), 8.
74. Japanese Trade Ministry Asks Firms to Prepare for ISO 14000, *International Environmental Systems Update,* 3(1), 1.
75. Japanese Firms Certify to ISO 14001 Despite Absence of National Program, *International Environmental Systems Update,* 3(6), 7.

76. **Gronner, Sam,** AT&T Helps EPA Streamline Regulatory Process, *Business Wire*, November 3, 1995.
77. **Fraust, C. L.,** Senior Staff Engineer, Lucent Technologies. Interview by author, Allentown, PA, August 1, 1996.
78. **Cascio, Joseph,** VP, Global Environment & Technology Foundation, Chair of U.S. Technical Advisory Group to the ISO, Interview by author, Annandale, VA, July 29, 1996.
79. **Poduska, Richard A.,** Director, Health, Safety & Environmental Affairs, Eastman Kodak Company, Interview by author, Rochester, NY, September 16, 1996.
80. **Potter, Julie,** Director, Corporate Environmental Affairs, Bausch & Lomb, Interview by author, Rochester, NY, April 1996.
81. **Potter, Julie,** Director, Corporate Environmental Affairs, Bausch & Lomb, Interview by author, Rochester, NY, April 1996.
82. **Sief, James, M.,** Secretary, Pennsylvania Department of Environmental Protection, ISO 14000 in the Next Generation of Environmental Protection Tools, Testimony before the Senate Environmental Resources and Energy Committee, March 20, 1996.
83. **Herman, Steven Al,** Assistant Administrator, USEPA, Office of Enforcement and Compliance Assurance, Internal memorandum to EPA Directors, June 25, 1996.
84. **USEPA,** Partnerships in Preventing Pollution, *100-B-96-001*, Spring 1996.
85. **USEPA,** Partnerships in Preventing Pollution, *100-B-96-001*, Spring 1996.
86. **USEPA,** Partnerships in Preventing Pollution, *100-B-96-001*, Spring 1996.
87. **President Bill Clinton and Vice President Al Gore,** Reinventing Environmental Regulation, Clinton Administration regulatory reform initiatives, March 16, 1995.
88. **USEPA,** Common Sense Strategies to Protect Public Health, a Progress Report on Reinventing Environmental Regulation, March 29, 1996.
89. **USEPA,** Notices: Regulatory Reinvention (XL) Pilot Projects, *Federal Register*, 60(99), 60 CFR17282, May 23, 1995.
90. **USEPA,** *Statement of Regulatory Priorities.* 60 CFR59658, November 20, 1995.
91. **USEPA,** Common Sense Strategies to Protect Public Health, a Progress Report on Reinventing Environmental Regulation, March 29, 1996.
92. **USEPA,** Project XL Frequently Asked Questions, Project XL Homepage, URL address: http://199.223.29.233/xl_home/xl_q&a/html.
93. **USEPA,** Project XL Frequently Asked Questions. Project XL Homepage, URL address: (http://199.223.29.233/xl_home/xl_q&a.html).
94. **Dombrowski, John,** USEPA Office of Enforcement and Compliance Assurance, Memorandum to Rosemary Maginniss, ANSI, August 20, 1996.
95. States Move to Coordinate ISO 14000 Pilot Project, *State Environmental Monitor*, 1(8), 13, 1996.
96. **McCreary, Jean H.,** ISO 14000: A Framework for Coordinating Existing Environmental Management Responsibilities, *Environmental Law & Practice*, January/February 1996, 38.
97. **Phillips, Earl W., Jr., and Freeman, Brian,** Privatizing Environmental Regulation: From Do-As-You're Told to Do-It-Yourself, *Connecticut Law Tribune*, November 13, 1995.
98. Pennsylvania Department of Environmental Protection Announces Voluntary Environmental Audit Policy, *PR Newswire*, September 25, 1996.
99. **Pedersen, William F., Jr.,** *Environmental Law Reporter*, September 1995.

100. **Howard, Philip K.,** *The Death of Common Sense: How Law is Suffocating America.* Tribune Books.
101. **President Bill Clinton and Vice President Al Gore,** Reinventing Environmental Regulation, Clinton Administration regulatory reform initiatives, March 16, 1995.
102. Chilton, Kenneth, Speakers at Cato Institute Seminar Agree Regulatory Change Needed, *Environmental Week,* 34(18), 1996.
103. Project XL: Minnesota's Enviro. Agency Suspends Program, *Greenwire,* August 29, 1996.
104. Minnesota, Charging EPA Input Inflexibility, Suspends its Pilot Project XL Efforts, *Environment Week,* 34(35), 1996.
105. Oversight: 3M, MPCA Protest EPA's Inflexibility of Companies Project XL Permit, *Hazardous Waste News,* 18(36), 1996.
106. Inflexibility? EPA Clings to Command and Control; 3M Shelves Project XL Proposal, *Environmental Remediation Technology,* 4(19), 1996.
107. 3M Quits Project XL, *Chemical Week,* 49, September 26, 1996.
108. Minnesota, Charging EPA Input Inflexibility, Suspends its Pilot Project XL Efforts, *Environment Week* 34(35), September 9, 1996.
109. **Fairley, Peter,** Frustrations with Project XL Mount, *Chemical Week,* 14, September 11, 1996.
110. House GOP Report Highly Critical of EPA's Efforts at Reinvention, *Environment Week,* 34(38), September 30, 1996.
111. Project XL: EPA Officials Move to Save Troubled Program, *Greenwire,* Spotlight story, December 4, 1996.
112. Project XL: EPA Officials Move to Save Troubled Program, *Greenwire,* Spotlight story, December 4, 1996.
113. **Powers, Mary Buckner,** Owners Drift From Voluntary Plan, *Engineering News-Record,* 237(24), 8, 1996.
114. States, Charging USEPA Bungled Project XL, Set Up Reform Group, *State Environmental Monitor,* 1(8), 3, 1996.
115. States, Charging USEPA Bungled Project XL, Set Up Reform Group, *State Environmental Monitor,* 1(8), 3, 1996.
116. States, Charging USEPA Bungled Project XL, Set Up Reform Group, *State Environmental Monitor,* 1(8), 3, 1996.
117. Audit Debate May Pivot on Showdown Between USEPA and Texas, *State Environmental Monitor,* 1(8), 4, 1996.
118. **Pascual, Pasky,** EPA. Telephone conversation with author, January 2, 1997.
119. **Pascual, Pasky,** EPA. Telephone conversation with author, January 2, 1997.
120. Compliance with legislation and regulatory requirements, *National Accreditation Program Criteria for Bodies Operating Registration of Environmental Management Systems,* Section 4.1.3.1, ANSI — RAB, September 1996.
121. **Pedersen, William F., Jr.,** *Environmental Law Reporter,* September 1995.
122. **Yandle, Bruce,** Environmental Policy: Thoughts on a Positive Agenda, *Vital Speeches,* 62(16), 510, 1996.
123. Reinventing Environmental Management, March 16, 1995.
124. *ISO 14001 Environmental Management Systems: Specifications with Guidance for Use,* Introduction, International Organization for Standardization, 1996.
125. ISO New Summaries, *IIS On-Line,* URL address: www.iso14000.org., March 21, 1997.
126. ISO New Summaries, *IIS On-Line,* URL address: www.iso14000.org., March 21, 1997.

127. **Hale, Greg,** ISO 14000 Accepted/Mandated, *IIS On-Line,* URL address: www.iso14000.org., March 20, 1997.
128. **Cascio, Joseph,** ISO 14000 Offers Environmental Protection Benefits, *International Environmental Systems Update,* 4(3), 2, CEEM, 1997.
129. **USEPA,** Incentives for Self-Policing: Discovery, Disclosure, Correction and Prevention of Violations, *Federal Register,* December 22, 1995.
130. **USEPA,** Statement of Policy: Incentives for Self-Policing, B. Definitions, *Federal Register,* 60(246), 66710, 1995.
131. 3M's Corporate Environmental Goals Evident in Home Repair Products, *PR Newswire,* March 14, 1995.
132. Green heat: pressures being experienced by the business sector to improve environmental performance, *MIT Alumni Assoc. Technology Review,* July 1995.
133. The House's Paean to Polluters, *Hartford Courant,* p. A10, August 2, 1995.
134. **Miller, George,** quoted by David Helvarg, Congress plans an American Clearcut: Defoliating our green laws, *The Nation,* 261(19), 699, 1995.
135. **Gunter, Booth,** GOP expected to press environmental overhaul, *The Tampa Tribune,* p. 2, January 2, 1997.
136. Congress: DeLay Adopts Moderate Tone on Environment, *Greenwire,* November 26, 1996.
137. **Hawkins, George S.,** Senior Advisor to the Office of Assistance and Pollution Prevention, U.S. Environmental Protection Agency, Region 1, The Eagle Agenda: An Agenda for the Future of Environmental Protection, p. 2, 1996.
138. **Hawkins, George S.,** Senior Advisor to the Office of Assistance and Pollution Prevention, U.S. Environmental Protection Agency, Region 1, The Eagle Agenda: An Agenda for the Future of Environmental Protection, p. 2, 1996.
139. Audit Debate May Pivot on Showdown Between USEPA and Texas. *State Environmental Monitor,* 1(8), 4, 1996.
140. EPA Officials Urge Regions to Step Up Traditional Enforcement in FY97, *Inside EPA Weekly Report,* 17(40), 1996.
141. **Gore, Al, Vice President,** Creating a Government that Works Better & Costs Less: Reinventing Environmental Management, *National Performance Review,* September 1993.
142. Editor's Page, *ES&T,* v.1(1), American Chemical Society (ACS), January 1967.
143. **Bown, Michael,** Environmental Agency Makes Sense, *ES&T,* 4(7), ACS, 1970.
144. **Sarnof, David,** Lake Erie, Dying but not Dead, *ES&T,* 1(3), ACS, 1967.
145. **Middleton, John T.,** A Fresh Opportunity for Industry, *ES&T,* 1(3), ACS, March 1967.
146. **Middleton, John T.,** Sulfur Oxides Must Be Controlled, *ES&T,* 4(2), ACS, 1970.
147. Environmental Currents, *ES&T,* 5(1), 1971.
148. Environmental Currents, *ES&T,* 5(1), 1971.
149. Environmental Currents, *ES&T,* 5(1), 1971.
150. Environmental Currents, *ES&T,* 5(1), 1971.
151. Environmental Currents, *ES&T,* 5(2), 1971.
152. Viewpoint, *ES&T,* 5(3), 1971.
153. Environmental Currents, *ES&T,* 5(4), 1971.
154. Environmental Currents, *ES&T,* 5(5), 1971.
155. Environmental Currents — Outlook, *ES&T,* 5(6), 1971.
156. **Bowen, Michael,** Editorial, *ES&T,* 5(12), 1971.
157. **Bowen, Michael,** Editorial, *ES&T,* 5(12), 1971.
158. Environmental Currents, *ES&T,* 6(8), 1972.

159. Environmental Currents, *ES&T,* 6(9), 1972.
160. **HMM,** Pollution Control's Man-in-the-middle, *ES&T,* 6(3), 216, 1972.
161. Anti-pollution effort taking ever larger share of U.S. GNP, *Commerce America,* 2(6), 15, 1977.
162. Abstracts, *The New York Times,* 76, March 31, 1973.
163. Interview, with Thomas W. Carmody, *ES&T,* 8(8), 1974.
164. Abstracts, *The New York Times,* 76, March 31, 1973.
165. Anti-pollution effort taking ever larger share of U.S. GNP, *Commerce America,* 2(6), 15, 1977.
166. **Hamrin, Robert,** Are environmental regulations hurting the economy?, *Challenge,* 8(2), 29, 1975.
167. **Train, Russell E.,** EPA aims to preserve profits while protecting the environment, *Commerce Today,* 6(4), 8, 1975.
168. Earth Day is no longer a street scene, *Chemical Week,* 37, April 23, 1975.
169. Earth Day is no longer a street scene, *Chemical Week,* 37, April 23, 1975.
170. **Sheridan, John H.,** Are controls leading us to nationalization?, *Industry Week,* 184(6), 21, 1975.
171. **Chastain, Clark E.,** Corporate accounting for environmental information, *Financial Executive,* 43(5), 45, 1975.
172. **Gibson, Charles H.,** Amortization of Pollution Control Facilities, *Ohio CPA Journal,* 37(4), 119, 1978.
173. **DeSanto, Robert S.,** Ed., *Environmental Management,* 1(1), 1976.
174. Anti-pollution effort taking ever larger share of U.S. GNP, *Commerce America,* 2(6), 15, 1977.
175. Economic Growth with Environmental Quality, *ES&T,* 11(2), 132, 1977.
176. **Bower, Blair T., Ehler, Charles N., and Kneese, Alan V.,** Incentives for Managing the Environment, *ES&T,* 11(3), 250, 1977.
177. Best control strategy in the bank, *Chemical Week,* 120(26), 42, June 29, 1977.
178. **Lawrence, Floyd G.,** Where on Earth does industry stand in pollution control?, *Industry Week,* 192(4), 42, February 14, 1977.
179. A bubble idea to stem pollution, *Business Week,* 2566, 42, December 25, 1978.
180. **Sheridan, John H.,** EPA Agenda: assault on toxics; rulemaking, *Industry Week,* 196(1), 19, 1978.
181. **Yandle, Bruce,** The emerging market in air pollution rights, *Regulation,* 2(4), 21, 1978.
182. ACS Updates Environmental Report, *Chemical & Engineering News,* 56(49), 34, 1978.
183. Antipollution spending takes a breather, *Chemical Week,* 122(20), 27, May 17, 1978.
184. **Kahalas, Harvey,** Ecology, Pollution and Business: A proposed planning solution, *Long Range Planning,* 11(6), 1978.
185. **Lovelock, J.E.,** *Gaia: A New Look at Life on Earth,* Oxford University Press, London, 1979.
186. OGJ Newsletter, *Oil & Gas Journal,* 4, April 16, 1979.
187. **Tucker, Lewis R., Jr.,** Profiling Environmentally Responsible Consumer-Citizens, *Journal of the Academy of Marketing Science,* 9(4), 454, 1981.
188. **Zim, Marvin, H.,** Allied Chemical's $20-Million Ordeal, *Fortune,* 98(5), 82, 1978.
189. Environmental managers face some solid problems, *Chemical Week,* 41, February 21, 1979.
190. **Levine, Richard,** Unfinished business: Reagan's Regulatory Relief. *Management Review,* American Management Association, 78(3), 18, 1989.

191. Midnight dumping: It still happens in large plants, *Chemical Week*, 41, February 21, 1981.
192. Battle Opens on Oil Spill Bills, *Platt's Oilgram News*, 59(48), 4, 1981.
193. **Levine, Richard,** Unfinished business: Reagan's Regulatory Relief, *Management Review*, American Management Association, 78(3), 18, 1989.
194. EPA Superfund Nominee Criticized by Environmental Groups at Senate Hearings, *Daily Report for Executives*, Bureau of National Affairs, 59, 1, March 26, 1982.
195. EPA Superfund Nominee Criticized by Environmental Groups at Senate Hearings, *Daily Report for Executives*, Bureau of National Affairs, 59, 1, 1982.
196. **Russakoff, Dale, and Sugawara, Sandra,** Reagan EPA Aids Change Tone, Not Tune, *The Washington Post*, A1, May 24, 1982.
197. Getting RCRA under control, *Chemical Week*, 36, June 9, 1982.
198. **Shabecoff, Philip,** EPA sets waste dumping rules for sites on land to protect water, *The New York Times*, p. A1, July 14, 1982.
199. **Royston, Michael G.,** Local and Multinational Corporations: Reappraising Environmental Management, *Environment*, 27(1), 12, 1985.
200. Getting RCRA under control, *Chemical Week*, 36, June 9, 1982.
201. **Royston, Michael G.,** Local and Multinational Corporations: Reappraising Environmental Management, *Environment*, 27(1), 12, 1985.
202. **Shabecoff, Philip,** EPA Declares Aide's Dismissal Wasn't Political, *The New York Times*, p. A1, February 10, 1983.
203. ALJ Approves Agreement Between EPA, Whistleblower, *Daily Report for Executives*, Bureau of National Affairs, 32, A-2, February 15, 1983.
204. **Hoffman, David and Peterson, Cass,** Burford Quits as EPA Administrator, *The Washington Post*, p. A1, March 10, 1983.
205. Ruckelshaus Nomination, *MacNeil/Lehrer Report*, March 21, 1983.
206. Burning Hazardous Waste, *Chemical Week*, p. 92, October 5, 1983.
207. **Freedman, Martin and Jaggi, Bikki,** Business and the Environment: Toward Common Ground (the SEC's pollution disclosure requirements, are they meaningful?), *Conservation Foundation Report 1984*, p. 405.
208. **Jackson, Tim,** Ed., *Clean Production Strategies*, Stockholm Environment Institute, Stockholm, 1993, p.167.
209. The Eighties in Review, *The New York Times*, December 24, 1989.
210. **Jackson, Tim,** Ed., *Clean Production Strategies*, Stockholm Environment Institute, Stockholm, 1993, p.166.
211. **Royston, Michael G.,** Local and Multinational Corporations: Reappraising Environmental Management, *Environment*, 27(1), 12, 1985.
212. **Royston, Michael G.,** Local and Multinational Corporations: Reappraising Environmental Management, *Environment*, 27(1), 12, 1985.
213. **Royston, Michael G.,** Local and Multinational Corporations: Reappraising Environmental Management, *Environment*, 27(1), 12, 1985.
214. **Royston, Michael G.,** Local and Multinational Corporations: Reappraising Environmental Management, *Environment*, 27(1), 12, 1985.
215. **Royston, Michael G.,** Local and Multinational Corporations: Reappraising Environmental Management, *Environment*, 27(1), 12, 1985.
216. The Eighties in Review, *The New York Times*, December 24, 1989.
217. **Rosenbaum, Bob,** Innovations in Waste Management Industry, *Business First — Buffalo*, (2)23, 8, 1986.

218. Hazardous waste handlers are going back to school, *Chemical Engineering*, p. 22, September 14, 1987.
219. **Luzzatto, Donald,** Social Investing: The Protest for the 1980's, *National Underwriter*, 91(4), 4, 1987.
220. **Garelik, Glenn,** A Breath of Fresh Air, *Time*, p. 35, September 28, 1987.
221. **Jackson, Tim,** Ed., *Clean Production Strategies*, Stockholm Environment Institute, Stockholm, 1993, p.167.
222. **Kiesche, Elizabeth,** Facing the Environmental Chill on Acquisitions, *Chemical Week*, 143(12), 26, September 21, 1988.
223. **Clark, William C.,** Ed., Environmental Priorities for the New President, *Environment*, 31(1), 5, 1989.
224. **Stavens, Robert N.,** Harnessing Market Forces to Protect the Environment, *Environment*, 31(1), 5, 1989.
225. **Kiesche, Elizabeth,** Facing the Environmental Chill on Acquisitions, *Chemical Week*, 143(12), 26, September 21, 1988.
226. **Clune, Ray,** New way to make vat dyes found by Sandoz Chemicals, *Daily New Record*, 18(198), 2, October 14, 1988.
227. **Breen, Barry,** Citizen Suits for Natural Resources Damages: Closing a Gap in Federal Environmental Law, *Wake Forest Law Review*, 24(4), 851, 1989.
228. **Smith, Andy,** Survey Claims Socially Selected Investments Can Provide Profitable Return, *Corporate Cashflow*, 10(4), 22, 1989.
229. **Kerr, John,** Smart answers for toxic troubles: answers to environmental affairs problems for electronic companies, *Electronic Business*, 15(19), 30, September 18, 1989.
230. Environmental Issue Management Moving to Heart of American Business Policies; New study profides insight on corporate attitudes, *Financial News*, October 30, 1990.
231. **Barnard, Jayne, W.,** Exxon Collides with the 'Valdez Principles', *Business & Society Review*, 74, 32, 1990.
232. **Sobel, Steven B.,** Challenge of the '90s, *Canadian Insurance*, 95(6), 22, 1990.
233. **Bostian, David B., Jr.,** Paradigms for Prosperity: Economic and Political Trends for the 1990 and Early 21st Century, *Futurist*, 24(4), 33, 1990.
234. **Silas, C.J.,** The Environment: Playing to Win, *Public Relations Journal*, 46(1), 10, 1990.
235. **Patterson, Timothy D.,** Preserving the Planet: A Mounting Problem, World, 24(1), 8, 1990.
236. **Rotman, David,** Environmental Regulation: How Mounting Public Pressures and New Legislation Will Reshape the Way Industry Does Business, *Chemical Week*, 145(13), 66, September 27, 1989.
237. **Rainey, John S.,** Innovative Energy, *Business & Economic Review*, 37(1), 39, 1990.
238. **Newall, J.E.,** Managing Environmental Responsibility, *Business Quarterly*, 55(2), 90, 1990.
239. **Barnard, Jayne, W.,** Exxon Collides with the 'Valdez Principles,' *Business & Society Review*, 74, 32, 1990.

Index

F

G

H

I

J

K

L

M

N

O

P

Q

R

S

T

U

V

W

X

Y